The GriefWork Companion

Activities for Healing

by Fran Zamore, MSW, ACSW & Ester Leutenberg

Illustrated by
Amy L. Brodsky, LISW-S

wholeperson
Stress & Wellness Publishers
Duluth, Minnesota

Whole Person Associates
101 W. 2nd St., Suite 203
Duluth, MN 55802

800-247-6789

books@wholeperson.com
www.wholeperson.com

The GriefWork Companion ~ Activities for Healing

Printed in the United States of America

10 9 8 7 6 5 4 3 2 1

Editorial Director: Carlene Sippola
Art Director: Joy Morgan Dey

Library of Congress Control Number: 2010929988
ISBN: 978-1-57025-240-2

DEDICATION

The GriefWork Companion ~ Activities for Healing
is dedicated to the memory of
**Joseph D. Zamore, Mae R. & Herman Zelikow,
Mitchell A. Leutenberg, Ethyl & Meyer Atkin and Alter Gottlieb**
whom we continue to love, and who continue to inspire us.

OUR THANKS & GRATITUDE

To our families for their support with this book and in our lives:

Children and their spouses –
Michael Zamore, Abigail Smith, Rachel Zamore, David Cohen and Judith Zamore
and grandchildren –
Emmett Smith Zamore, Henry Smith Zamore and Elias Jacob Zamore-Cohen

Husband Jay Leutenberg,
Daughters and their husbands –
Amy and Jack Brodsky, Kathy and Siri-Dya Khalsa and Lynne and David Yulish
and grandchildren –
Kyle Jacob, Tyler Mitchell and Evan Daniel Brodsky
Shayna Livia, Arielle Liat and Mason Leutenberg Korb,
Moselle Hannah, Avidan Yosef and Yishai Gavriel Yulish,

To the following whose input we truly appreciate:

Kenneth J. Doka, PhD
Joanettia E. Grier, MS, MA
Margaret Hadley, RN, MSN
Kathy Atarah Khalsa, MAJS, OTR/L
Jay L. Leutenberg
Anne Mazonson, M.D.

Franca S. Posner, MSW, LCSW-C, LICSW, CT
Eileen Regen, M.Ed., CJE
Mary K. Robitaille, RN, BSN, MS
John Slavcoff
Mary Ann Staky
Roberta Tonti, LISW, ACSW, BCD, IMFT

*To Amy L. Brodsky, LISW-S, whose creative, thoughtful illustrations
give our words reality and added meaning.*

To all the participants, volunteers and colleagues at
NCJW/Montefiore Hospice in Beachwood, Ohio and
Holy Cross Home Care and Hospice in Silver Spring, Maryland
who shared their thoughts and feelings freely and have taught so much!

**To each other for friendship, support, encouragement,
tears and laughter throughout the years!**

Ester & Fran

TABLE OF CONTENTS

TABLE OF CONTENTS

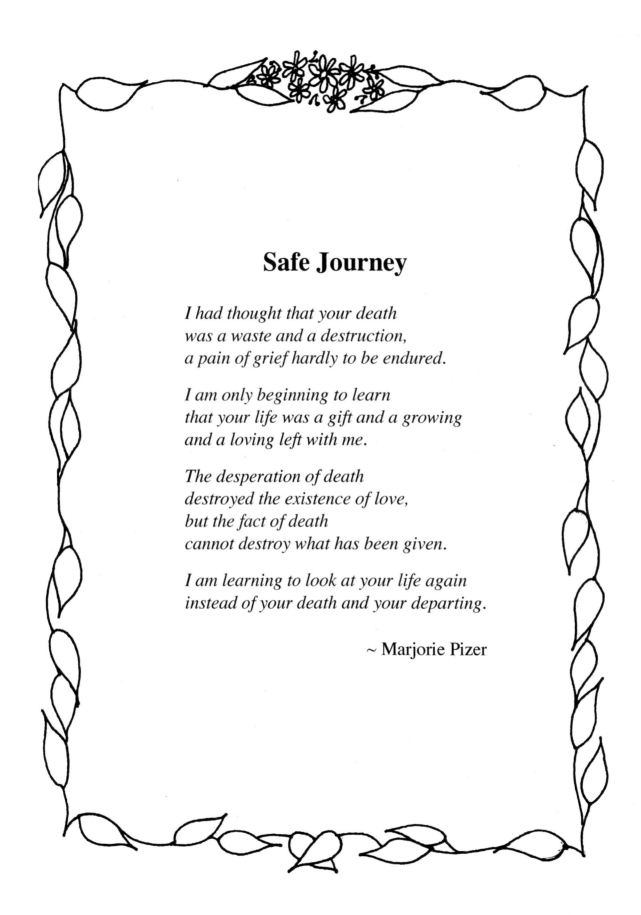

Safe Journey

I had thought that your death
was a waste and a destruction,
a pain of grief hardly to be endured.

I am only beginning to learn
that your life was a gift and a growing
and a loving left with me.

The desperation of death
destroyed the existence of love,
but the fact of death
cannot destroy what has been given.

I am learning to look at your life again
instead of your death and your departing.

~ Marjorie Pizer

Introduction

to

The GriefWork Companion
~ Activities for Healing

This section provides important background information.

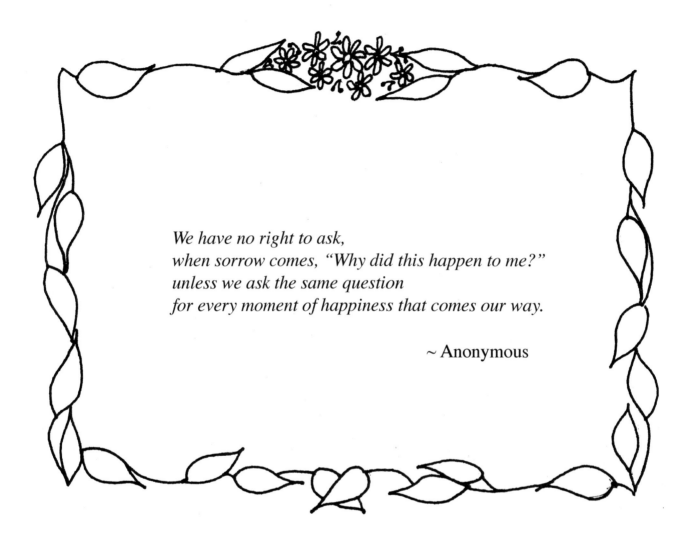

We have no right to ask,
when sorrow comes, "Why did this happen to me?"
unless we ask the same question
for every moment of happiness that comes our way.

~ Anonymous

About *The GriefWork Companion*
~ Activities for Healing

Through our work and drawing from our personal experiences, we have become fully aware of the complexities associated with grieving. We live in a society where people are expected to 'get-over' their loss quickly and we understand this is not realistic. We know there are many ways that people grieve and we support each person's right to grieve in an individual and unique fashion.

The GriefWork Companion was developed to help men and women heal from their losses. Everyone experiences loss. We refer to the process of coping with a significant loss as grief work. The typical range of behaviors, emotions and attitudes is varied. Throughout the book we try to convey that everyone's grief has a unique expression.

The GriefWork Companion contains activities and thought-provoking quotations as well as educational and journaling pages. Not all activities are applicable for everyone. Use those which seem appropriate and relevant for you.

Journaling is a time-honored way to help people sort out their thoughts and feelings. Many different techniques can be used to begin a journaling practice. One way is to set aside some time each day – maybe 15 to 30 minutes in the morning – to simply write whatever comes to mind. Another way is to pick up a journal and write when you have a 'thinking loop' that seems stuck. In the act of writing, often the thought or situation will lose its intensity. Some people find that journaling is a substitute for 'talking' and others use their journals as a way of writing letters to the person who is no longer present. Journaling can be just as effective if it is brief, or if it is lengthy, as long as it reflects how you are currently feeling.

Many people find that they are surprised at how their thinking has evolved when they re-read their journals. For most people the changes that they are experiencing are subtle. Often people grieving do not realize the hard work that they have done, nor do they recognize the changes they have made. Re-reading a journal can provide an opportunity for self-appreciation.

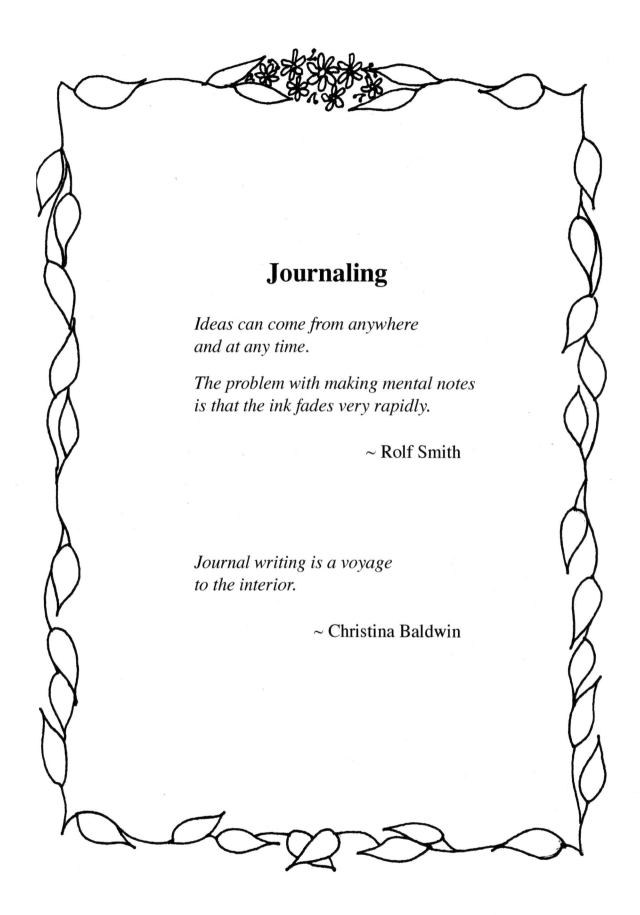

Journaling

*Ideas can come from anywhere
and at any time.*

*The problem with making mental notes
is that the ink fades very rapidly.*

~ Rolf Smith

*Journal writing is a voyage
to the interior.*

~ Christina Baldwin

The Grief Experience

One of the important aspects of grieving that has been largely overlooked is the relational aspect. Each person's grief is unique because the person . . .

- Had a unique relationship with the deceased (loving, ambivalent, challenging)
- Brings a unique personality and way of coping to the situation
- Has a particular world view which will impact how to enter the process
- Has ongoing relationships which may or may not be helpful
- Has a unique attitude about death
- Came to this particular loss with a personal history of dealing with earlier losses
- Has particular expectations about what dealing with the loss means and wonders how to proceed

The grieving process can occur with many types of losses; although we focus on loss by death, the concepts presented can be applied to other losses. See pages 12 and 13 for a partial listing of other losses.

We view the grieving experience as a long, winding path that curves back on itself, traverses hills and valleys and has many obstacles. It is a path that is challenging to negotiate and time-consuming to travel along. This provides opportunities for personal and spiritual growth. Because grieving is part of the human experience, a person attached to someone will mourn the loss of that relationship and miss that person's physical presence. We understand this as a simple truth. Remembering this truth helps some people cope with the loss because they are able to be somewhat philosophical.

The process may be more complicated when the relationship with the deceased was either ambivalent or challenging. The reality for most people is that relationships are not easy to put into categories. Most long-standing relationships are at times loving, at times ambivalent and at times challenging. The degree of challenge will likely add to the complex feelings that the person who is grieving will experience. Along with the death of the person, the bereaved may also grieve the reality of needs that were not met with that person during his/her lifetime.

Definitions

LOSS refers to no longer having somebody or something.

GRIEF is the universal response to any loss.

BEREAVEMENT refers to the experience of the loss of someone through death.

MOURNING refers to the expression of grief in culturally specific ways.

Kinds of Losses

Loss is a part of everyone's life at one point or another. Each individual reacts to a loss in a personal way. As well as the emotional-evoking responses, loss also has physical, intellectual, behavioral, social and philosophical dimensions. Response to loss is varied and influenced by beliefs and practices.

People's losses, no matter who or what, are important and often devastating to them. They represent the disappearance of someone or something cherished.

Some examples of loss:

- Addiction
- Break Up/Divorce
- Death
- Employment
- End of a relationship
- Failed business venture
- Faith
- Financial security
- Health
- Home
- Independence
- Mental ability
- Pet
- Physical ability
- Plans, hopes and dreams
- Role in life
- Sense of safety/security
- Status
- Treasured possessions

Disenfranchised Grief

Disenfranchised grief refers to grief experiences not openly acknowledged, socially accepted or publicly mourned. Several circumstances may contribute to this phenomenon:

- The relationship is not recognized or validated, i.e., friend, co-worker, former spouse, in-law, same-sex partner, lover
- The loss is not recognized, i.e., prenatal (miscarriage, stillborn, abortion), infant death, aged parent, pet
- The person grieving is not acknowledged, i.e., young children, people with developmental disabilities, elderly with dementia
- Unusual circumstances of the death, i.e., suicide, violence, accident
- The stigma of mental illness, suicide, AIDS, alcoholism or drug addiction

Talking with a trusted friend or professional can be helpful for a person suffering from disenfranchised grief. One should not underestimate the value of having support during this healing journey.

"every society has norms that frame grieving . . .
When a family member dies, one is allowed
and expected to grieve, often in a specified way.
Yet human beings . . . harbor attachments to
fellow humans, animals and even places and things.
In situations (which are outside the grieving rules) . . .
the person experiences a loss, but the resulting grief
is unrecognized by others. The person has no socially
accorded right to grieve that loss or mourn it in a
particular way, the grief is disenfranchised"

~ Disenfranchised Grief
by Kenneth J. Doka, PhD

What I Learned About Grief

Today it's called "Disenfranchised Grief." In 1995 I called it lonely.

My mother lived with our family for 35 years. I call my husband a Saint for many reasons, but that's at the top of the list. Mom was a charitable woman who had an unhappy childhood. She was a self-concerned woman. When my boyfriend, the Saint, was 16, she asked him never to allow me to put her in a skilled care facility. As her Alzheimer's was progressing we knew we had no choice. And of course, she was angry – actually furious – at me, her only child.

After a few months, she stopped yelling and biting me, and didn't know anyone or where she was. For two years she screamed at everyone or no one – just screamed. I went to the facility twice a day for those two years, mainly to make sure she was being well cared for, which was no pleasure for her caregivers. I was tired, worn down and so very sad. My worse moment was when she stopped caring that the baseball game was on – her favorite! Her dignity and pride were gone. It was terrible. Alzheimer's is an awful disease.

After two weeks of watching her lie in bed, not opening her eyes, her nurse said to her, "It's OK to let go" and she sat up, opened her eyes and said "I'll die when I'm damn well ready," lay back down and died two weeks later. Earlier in the day that she died I had spent hours with the Alzheimer's unit administrator arguing. They were keeping her alive and I felt it was torturing her. We had all of the proper papers, I was her guardian – but this administrator's religious beliefs had kept my mom alive for those many weeks.

About 5 o'clock p.m. I received a phone call that my mom had died. My husband was at a business meeting. No cell phones. I had NO idea of where he was. I called my three daughters and they were all busy and unavailable to join me. In fairness to them, we all knew this was coming and they probably thought I could handle this alone, just as I had always handled everything, and I would be fine. Because my mother was 89 years old, and had lived a full life, I believe that it was expected that I would not need the support that one would usually receive for a loved one. But in truth, I wasn't fine. So I went alone to say goodbye to my mom. I kissed her and told her she put up a great fight, (she did NOT want to die!) and that her hands and her skin were still beautiful. I told that I loved her.

I NEVER felt so lonely in my life. Not when my father died when I was 15 years old, not when my son died by suicide, not ever. I wasn't angry – I was hurting. Even when my husband came home, even the next day when the girls came over, I felt like no one 'got it.' I felt so lonely. I've forgiven them – but there is no way I can forget that feeling of being so very alone. Though she was almost ninety, though she was a pain sometimes, though she had dementia, though for years she was not "my mom," I had now lost my mother.

I guess this is disenfranchised grief.

~ Anonymous

When to Seek Additional Support

This book is designed to help you deal with usual or common grief reactions. The pain, loneliness, sadness and distress that accompany grief are to be expected. Asking for and accepting additional support is a positive action that can truly be beneficial. You may want to seek out the help of friends, family, physicians, clergy and/or mental health professionals.

By its very nature, grieving is isolating. When we grieve we often are alone with our thoughts and memories. Although grief reactions are universal, most individuals feel alone and do not think others experience similar feelings. We strongly encourage anyone who is grieving to seek out a support group. Not all groups are created equal. Use your good judgment and participate in a group that feels comfortable and safe for you; where you feel supported and connected to others. The benefits of having time set aside to be with and talk with others, about the grieving experience can be enormous, giving you an emotional connection that may be valuable to improve your mood and attitude, and to decrease emotional distress.

Please recognize that symptoms of clinical depression and grieving are very similar. Sleep disturbances, appetite changes and intense sadness are common to both depression and grief. Depression is also characterized by a significant loss of self-esteem, a symptom not particularly common in usual grief reactions. If you are having prolonged periods of inability to manage daily tasks of living, if you feel hopeless and helpless and/or are preoccupied with guilt, it would be wise to consult with a mental health professional.

If you have suicidal thoughts you should seek professional help immediately. The National Suicide Prevention Lifeline telephone number is 1-800-273-8255.

(Continued on the next page)

When to Seek Additional Support *(Continued)*

People experiencing very difficult grief reactions, clinical depression or other significant mental health issues need to seek qualified professional help. Many factors may contribute to complicating grief, which can cause complicated grief reactions. These reactions are all legitimate.

Some contributing factors:

- An estranged or overly dependent relationship with the deceased
- Your own underlying mental health issues
- Social isolation
- Sudden and traumatic circumstances of the death
- Concurrent life crisis which may lead to a delayed grief reaction
- Personal history of poor coping with prior losses
- Substance abuse or addictions of any kind
- Disenfranchised grief (page 13)

Be aware that these complicating factors do not necessarily lead to complicated grief – they are 'red flags.'

Pay attention to the degree and duration of your intense sadness when determining if you think you are suffering from a complicated grief or depression. If, over time (months, not weeks) your grief symptoms are not lessening, seek support. Healing is a long, slow process. Be gentle with yourself and do not rush the process. If you are uncomfortable, seek support and the help you need.

Continuing Bonds

(After-Death Communications – Extraordinary Experiences)

The idea of continuing bonds after the death of a loved one is fascinating. Many people maintain their connection by sharing memories, continuing particular activities and/or memorializing their loved one in a variety of ways.

Dreaming, sensing the loved one's presence, smelling a particular fragrance, having the sensation of being gently touched, are some examples of continuing bonds that are referred to as after-death communications or extraordinary experiences. These phenomena are fairly common and experienced as pleasant, positive, loving encounters. However, not everyone experiences these events.

Often times, people who have extraordinary experiences or after death communications with their loved ones are uncomfortable discussing them with others. If you have had any such experiences, you may want to journal about them.

Life After Death

The things I know:
    How the living go on living
    and how the dead go on living with them
so that in a forest
    even a dead tree casts a shadow
    and the leaves fall one by one
and the branches break in the wind
and the bark peels off slowly
and the trunk cracks
    and the rain seeps in through the cracks
and the trunk falls to the ground
and the moss covers it
    and in the spring the rabbits find it
and build their nest inside
and have their young
and their young will live safely
inside the dead tree
so that nothing is wasted in nature
    or in love.

~ Laura Gilpin

How Do You Handle Adversity?

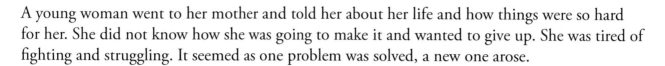

Are you a Carrot, an Egg or a Coffee Bean?

A young woman went to her mother and told her about her life and how things were so hard for her. She did not know how she was going to make it and wanted to give up. She was tired of fighting and struggling. It seemed as one problem was solved, a new one arose.

Her mother took her in the kitchen. She filled three pots with water and placed each on a high fire. Soon the pots came to a boil. In the first, she placed carrots, in the second she placed eggs, and the last she placed ground coffee beans. She let them sit and boil, without saying a word.

In about twenty minutes, she turned off the burners. She fished the carrots out and placed them in a bowl. She pulled the eggs out and placed them in a bowl. Then she ladled the coffee out and placed it in a bowl.

Turning to her daughter, she asked, "Tell me, what do you see?"

"Carrots, eggs and coffee," she replied. Her mother brought her closer and asked her to feel the carrots. She did and noted that they were soft. The mother then asked her to take an egg and break it. After pulling off the shell, she observed the hard boiled egg. Finally, the mother asked the daughter to sip the coffee. The daughter smiled, as she tasted it and noticed its rich aroma. The daughter then asked, "What does it mean, Mother?"

She explained that each of these objects had faced the same adversity – boiling water. Each reacted differently. The carrot went in strong, hard, and unrelenting. However, after being subjected to the boiling water, it softened and became weak. The egg had been fragile. Its thin outer shell had protected its liquid interior, but after sitting in boiling water, its insides became hardened. The round coffee beans were unique, however. After they were in the boiling water, they had changed the water.

"Which are you?" she asked her daughter. "When adversity knocks on your door, how do you respond? Are you a carrot, an egg or a coffee bean?"

Think of this: Which are you? Are you the carrot that seems strong, but with pain and adversity do you wilt, become soft and lose your strength? Are you the egg that starts with a malleable heart, but changes with the heat? Do you have a fluid spirit, but after a death, breakup, a financial hardship, or some other trial, have you become hardened and stiff? Does your shell look the same, but on the inside are you bitter and tough, with a stiff spirit and hardened heart?

Or are you like the coffee bean? The bean actually changed the hot water, the very circumstances that bring the pain. When the water gets hot, it releases the fragrance and the flavor. If you are like the bean, when things are at their worst you get better and change the situation around you. When the hour is the darkest and trials are their greatest, do you elevate yourself to another level? How do you handle adversity? Are you a carrot, an egg or a coffee bean?

~ Anonymous

Your Healing Journey

As you embark on the activities in this book, you will find it useful to have a separate journal to continue recording your thoughts and feelings.

We wish you well on your healing journey.

Ester & Fran

People in Mourning

*People in mourning have to come to grips with death
    before they can live again.*

Mourning can go on for years and years.

It doesn't end after a year, that's a false fantasy.

*It usually ends when people realize
    that they can live again,
    that they can concentrate their energies
    on their lives as a whole,
    and not on their hurt, and guilt, and pain.*

~ Elisabeth Kübler-Ross

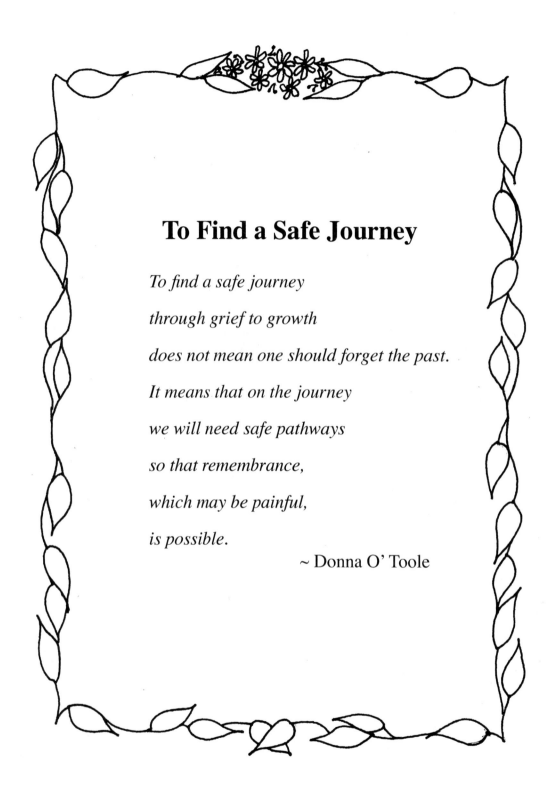

To Find a Safe Journey

To find a safe journey

through grief to growth

does not mean one should forget the past.

It means that on the journey

we will need safe pathways

so that remembrance,

which may be painful,

is possible.

~ Donna O' Toole

CHAPTER 1

Let's Get Started

The purpose of this chapter is to lay the foundation
for your healing journey.

Remembering the person I have loved allows me to slowly heal.
Healing does not mean I will forget. Actually, it means I will remember.
Gently, I will move forward, never forgetting my past.

~Alan D. Woldfelt, Ph.D., C.T.

About . . .

Permissions
and Ground Rules

We live in a society where people are expected to 'get-over' their loss quickly. This is not realistic! People grieve in many ways. In this book we support and honor each person's right to grieve in an individual and unique fashion. This page is designed to help you remember that you are unique, your relationship with your loved one was, and remains, unique and you are entitled to your unique way of grieving.

On the facing page . . .

Read the reminders which give you permission to grieve as well as help you manage your grief.

After completing the activity . . .

Select one or more of these quotes and journal your thoughts.

To spare oneself from grief at all costs can be achieved only at the price of total detachment, which excludes the ability to experience happiness.

~ Erich Fromm

Pain is only bearable if we know it will end, not if we deny it exists.

~ Viktor Frankl

Adversity often activates a strength we did not know we had.

~ Joan Walsh Anglund

_____

_____

_____

_____

_____

_____

_____

_____

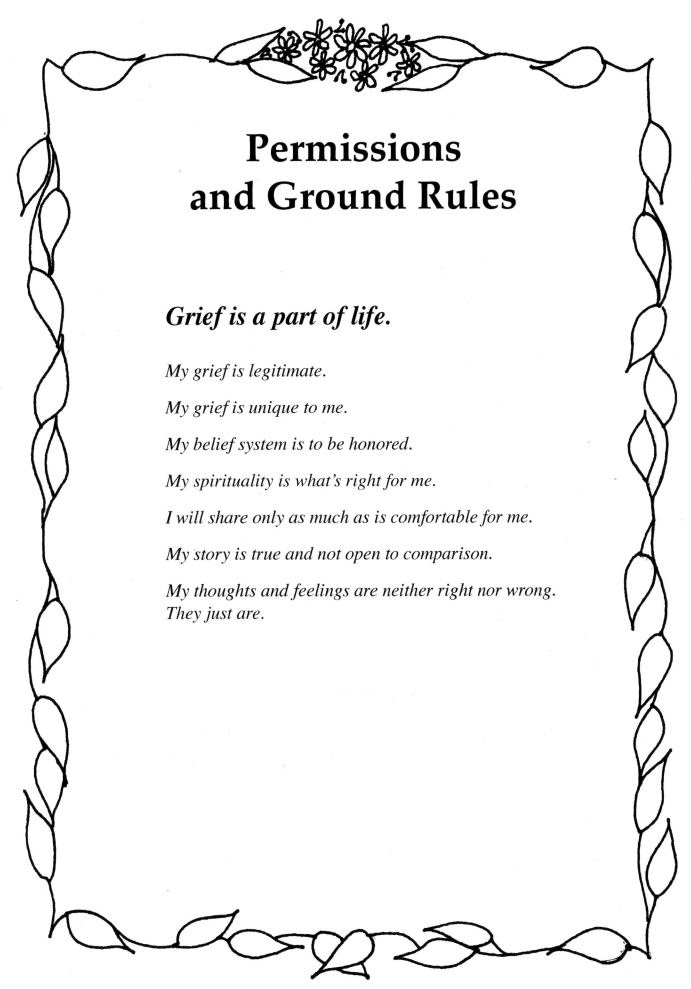

Permissions and Ground Rules

Grief is a part of life.

My grief is legitimate.

My grief is unique to me.

My belief system is to be honored.

My spirituality is what's right for me.

I will share only as much as is comfortable for me.

My story is true and not open to comparison.

My thoughts and feelings are neither right nor wrong. They just are.

About . . .

Ribbon Activity

This activity is a way to identify where you are in the grieving process and to notice who you are thinking about. Often, when we grieve, other people come to mind and we find ourselves grieving for them also.

On the facing page . . .

Imagine that each ribbon in the basket represents a different aspect of the grief process.

In your mind's eye, select the ribbon that is related to how you are feeling today and what is meaningful to you now. You may select more than one ribbon, and you may be thinking about more than one person as you select ribbons. If you wish, color in your selected ribbons.

Return to this activity in several months to see if there has been a shift.

After completing the activity . . .

Journal your thoughts and reasons for your color selections.

_____

_____

_____

_____

_____

_____

_____

_____

_____

_____

Ribbon Activity

The ribbon colors and their meanings are:

BLACK   Recent loss, active mourning

PURPLE   Transition, early stage of moving forward

GREEN   Healing, moving forward

BLUE   Anniversary of the loss or another memory trigger

About . . .

THE HEALING PATHWAY

The purpose of THE HEALING PATHWAY is to provide a framework for talking about the grieving experience without timelines or judgment.

The healing process is a journey: as the shock of the loss wears off and you start to experience your emotions fully and learn to manage them, you will begin to reorganize your life without your loved one's physical presence. As this healing occurs, you will have times when you find that you are dealing again with very intense feelings and think that you are back at the beginning of the process. We liken this to a path that keeps curving back on itself - with twists, turns and obstacles along the way.

The first experience along THE HEALING PATHWAY is that of *shock*. The numbness that is associated with this can be very useful. This is the time when you may have been on autopilot to manage life's tasks. In addition to numbness, *shock* is often characterized by disbelief that the loss actually occurred, and searching behavior (looking for the loved one in crowds or familiar places) is quite common.

Shock gradually wears off and as that is happening and reality sinks in, people move to a phase we call *disorganization*. This is 'the pits.' It is the phase that takes the longest to emerge from and is the place which everyone who grieves returns to time and time again, with diminishing intensity and duration. Holidays, birthdays, and other special occasions may flip you back; these setbacks will not be as intense nor will they last as long as previous setbacks. *Disorganization* is characterized by feeling the full impact of the loss. Yearning, missing, sadness, heavy-heartedness are all common. Some people also experience relief, fear of life without the loved one, and/or anger at needing to face the world without the loved one.

It is also during *disorganization* that people have difficulty concentrating and/or remembering, and they feel frustrated with themselves because they cannot seem to complete tasks they once managed with ease. Accidents are likely to happen during this phase as reflexes are diminished. Other common physical symptoms of disorganization include interrupted sleep patterns, appetite changes, general lethargy and a suppressed immune system. The good news is that this in not a permanent state. *Disorganization* leads to the next phase, *reorganization*. The lines between these two phases are fluid, and there is a great deal of going back and forth.

Reorganization is characterized by emerging from the fog of *disorganization*. This is when some people are able to consciously decide that they will take the experience of loss and grieving and use it as an impetus for their personal growth.

During the period of *reorganization*, you will be able to return to previous levels of functioning and may develop a new sense of purpose in life.

Active grieving will dissipate over time. Memories of the loved one will remain. As you journey on THE HEALING PATHWAY you will learn how to experience your emotions, relish your memories, and move on.

The purpose of THE HEALING PATHWAY is to help you establish your NEW NORMAL. NEW NORMAL refers to your ability to live life fully and with joy, without the physical presence of the person who died.

After reading the facing page . . .

Refer to this page frequently as a reminder of the twists and turns on your healing journey.

THE HEALING PATHWAY

The journey from *Loss* to *New Normal*
is a long, winding and complicated one.
You will recognize markers along the way that
help you to better understand the characteristics
of the phases of the grieving process.

SHOCK - THE REALITY OF THE LOSS HAS NOT SUNK IN

Some symptoms of SHOCK:
- Disbelief
- Euphoria
- Numbness
- Searching
- Suicidal thoughts*

DISORGANIZATION - FEELING THE IMPACT OF THE LOSS

Some symptoms of DISORGANIZATION:
- Aimlessness
- Anger
- Anguish
- Anxiety
- Apathy
- Avoidance
- Confusion
- Depression
- Fear
- Forgetfulness
- Guilt
- Hopelessness
- Isolation
- Loneliness
- Loss of appetite
- Loss of faith
- Loss of interest
- Loss of meaning
- Nightmares
- Physical distress
- Preoccupation
- Relief
- Restlessness
- Sadness
- Sleeplessness
- Slowed reaction time
- Suicidal thoughts*
- Yearning

REORGANIZATION - REBUILDING A SATISFYING LIFE – *New Normal*

Some symptoms of REORGANIZATION:
- Changed values
- Control over remembering
- Emergence of balanced memories
- New choices
- New meaning in life
- New priorities
- Pleasure in remembering
- Return to previous levels of functioning

These symptoms are NOT checklists. These lists represent *some* of the symptoms that *some* people feel *some* of the time. Every person's experience of grief is different and each has different feelings and reactions. Remember, THE HEALING PATHWAY is not a one-way or one-lane path. There is potential for a great deal of movement among the phases as we move towards a *New Normal*, which is constantly changing.

* If you have suicidal thoughts, seek professional help immediately.
The National Suicide Prevention Life-line telephone number is 1-800-273-8255.

About . . .

THE HEALING PATHWAY

The journey from *Loss* to *NEW NORMAL* is a long, winding and complicated one.

On the facing page . . .

The blank HEALING PATHWAY can be used for notes to mark your progress and pitfalls of your unique journey. You might want to use 'sticky-notes and move them along the path as circumstances change.

After completing the activity . . .

Reflect on this poem by Cinthia G. Kelley:

Grief Is Like a River

My grief is like a river, I have to let it flow,
but I myself determine just where the banks will go.

Some days the current takes me in waves of guilt and pain,
but there are always quiet pools where I can rest again.

I crash on rocks of anger; my faith seems faint indeed,
but there are other swimmers who know that what I need

Are loving hands to hold me when the waters are too swift,
and someone kind to listen when I just seem to drift.

Grief's river is a process of relinquishing the past.
By swimming in hope's channels, I'll reach the shore at last.

Journal your thoughts on the above poem or the following quotation by Kirsti A. Dyer, MD, MS, FT:

The path to healing from a loss is different for each person, one which may have unexpected twists and turns, but a road that has been traveled by many.

_____

_____

_____

_____

_____

_____

THE HEALING PATHWAY

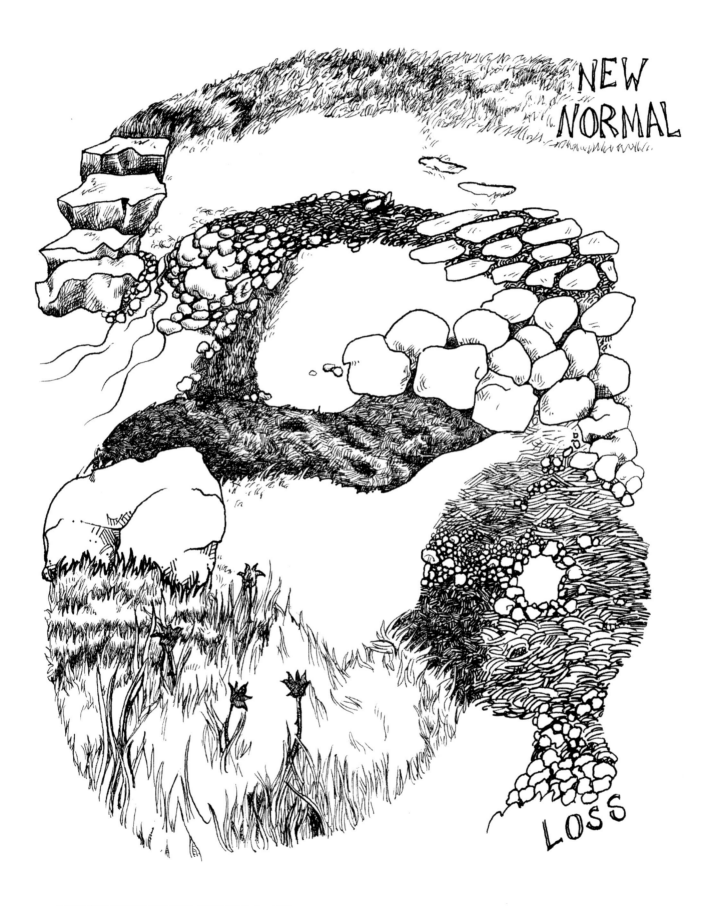

NEW NORMAL

LOSS

About . . .

TASKS OF HEALING FROM A LOSS

This page coordinates with THE HEALING PATHWAY, reminding you of the twists and turns of your path, and that it is not a one-way street. These are the tasks necessary to move to your *New Normal*.

Again, by *New Normal*, we are referring to your unique experience. *New Normal* is not a static destination and is unique to you. Each person has a unique way of being in the world. Your *New Normal* will be what is right for you. Any other's *New Normal* will be what is right for them. The goal is to develop a *New Normal* for yourself – a relatively comfortable way of living without the physical presence of the deceased. One's *New Normal* will continue to shift because it is a dynamic process of growth and change.

On the facing page . . .

Read the four tasks of healing.

After reading the facing page...

Journal your thoughts on this quotation from Walter Anderson:

> *I can choose to sit in perpetual sadness, immobilized by the gravity of my loss, or I can choose to rise from the pain and treasure the most precious gift I have – life itself.*
>
> ~ Walter Anderson

_____

_____

_____

_____

_____

_____

_____

_____

_____

TASKS OF HEALING FROM A LOSS

Four tasks are related to the work of grieving.
Personal growth and healing are built on these tasks.

ACCEPTING THE LOSS is the starting point for the work of grieving. Accepting the loss refers not only to intellectual acceptance, but to emotional recognition. Intellectual acceptance occurs as a person emerges from *shock*. The full emotional acceptance may take longer and occurs as the other tasks are being accomplished.

FEELING THE FEELINGS is counter-intuitive for most people. Most people would rather deny feelings, push them aside, distract themselves and/or 'stuff' them instead of experiencing the full weight of any uncomfortable feelings. Experiencing feelings is essential to the healing process. This is a primary task during *disorganization*.

ADJUSTING relates to learning to live without the presence of a loved one. Reorganizing one's life without the deceased depends on the nature of the relationship and role with the deceased. We associate this process with the stage of *reorganization* along THE HEALING PATHWAY.

MOVING FORWARD is when the grieving person has been able to adjust in a way that allows for personal growth. Moving forward does not imply forgetting. It is recognition of living life fully, being grateful for loved ones and all that we do have, with a genuine capacity for joy, in a newly constituted way and formulating a vision for the future. This coincides with the concept of *NEW NORMAL*.

About . . .

Mourners' Rights

This page is designed to help you understand your rights and normalize your experience. Since grieving is a new experience or situation, and because emotions are raw, it is sometimes confusing to know what is okay while mourning. It is important to remember that you do not need to live up to others' expectations.

On the facing page . . .

Read your rights.

After you have read the page . . .

Think of additional rights that you have – or rights you wish you could have – and jot them below.

_____

_____

_____

_____

_____

_____

_____

_____

_____

_____

_____

_____

_____

Mourners' Rights

- I have the right to experience my own unique grief in my own unique way.
- I have the right to feel what I am feeling, regardless of how those feelings shift from moment to moment.
- I have the right to feel angry.
- I have the right to be treated as a capable person.
- I have the right to say NO.
- I have the right to privacy.
- I have the right to ask for help.
- I have the right to be listened to.
- I have the right to be treated with respect.
- I have the right to socialize when ready.
- I have the right to cry – or not.
- I have the right to express my feelings – or not.
- I have the right to be upset.
- I have the right to be supported.
- I have the right to express my needs.
- I have the right to talk about my grief.
- I have the right to experience joy.
- I have the right to feel a multitude of emotions – or not.
- I have the right to be tolerant of my physical and emotional limits.
- I have the right to experience unexpected bursts of grief.
- I have the right to make use of healing rituals, including the funeral.
- I have the right to embrace my spirituality.
- I have the right to have fun.
- I have the right to be disappointed.
- I have the right to search for meaning in life and death.
- I have the right to treasure my memories.
- I have the right to be alone.
- I have the right to be given time for the healing process.

adapted from *My Mourners Bill of Rights* by Alan D. Wolfelt, Ph.D.

Never, never, never give up.

~ Winston Churchill

CHAPTER 2

Getting in Touch

Before people can move through their feelings, they need to know what they are experiencing. The purpose of this chapter is to help you recognize and acknowledge those feelings. Many people believe that the best way to cope with unpleasant feelings is to ignore or 'stuff' them. This is not true. In spite of the counter-intuitive nature of this, people need to be encouraged to sit with and feel what they are feeling. The more this happens, the greater the likelihood that you will recognize that feelings wax-and-wane, and the capacity for pleasant feelings exists *alongside* of difficult ones.

About . . .
GriefWork Emotions

You are capable of experiencing a wide variety of emotions at any given time. Recognizing this can be empowering. You will begin to appreciate just how challenging the grieving process can be when you take time to notice the different emotions you feel and the fact that you can experience any number of them at the same time. The intensity of your grief will subside over time; however, the grieving process does not happen in a step-by-step or orderly fashion. This page is an excellent reference sheet for many of the pages in this book.

On the facing page . . .

Check the emotions you are experiencing right now. At various times in the next few days, repeat this exercise, checking off with another mark or different color markers. You might want to track the time of day these feelings emerge. A particular emotion may be of significance to you in your disrupted life routine. It might heighten your awareness of specific times of the day that are best for you or it might help you notice particularly vulnerable times of the day. This emphasizes the point that people feel different emotions constantly – many at the same time – many in the same day. When you allow yourself to fully experience what you are feeling, the emotions tend to shift, sometimes slightly and sometimes dramatically.

One of the challenges is to notice your emotions without judging them or identifying with them. If you sit quietly and feel what you are feeling without any judgment about that particular feeling, you may actually be able to watch it shift into something else.

After completing the activity . . .

In what ways have you recently felt sad, restless or confused? Journal about it.

_____

_____

_____

_____

_____

_____

_____

GriefWork Emotions

"I feel ..."

Cautious ❑	Annoyed ❑	Loved ❑	Lonely ❑	Discouraged ❑	Jealous ❑
Frustrated ❑	Helpless ❑	Hostile ❑	Apathetic ❑	Disappointed ❑	Numb ❑
Relieved ❑	Confused ❑	Restless ❑	Sad ❑	Judged ❑	Hysterical ❑
Hopeless ❑	Guilty ❑	Anxious ❑	Angry ❑	Forgetful ❑	Regretful ❑
Disconnected ❑	Miserable ❑	Unsupported ❑	Yearning ❑	Shocked ❑	Capable ❑
Aimless ❑	Denial ❑	Acceptance ❑	Fear ❑	Hopeful ❑	Determined ❑
Supported ❑	Unfocussed ❑	Overwhelmed ❑	Needy ❑	Resilient ❑	Abandoned ❑

About . . .
The Emotions Salad Bowl

Recognizing the variety of simultaneous emotions can be empowering. You will begin to appreciate how challenging the grieving process can be when you notice the array of emotions you experience. In the salad bowl metaphor, variety is the 'spice of life.' You will become aware and recognize the different emotions you feel, all at the same time. Just as the wide variety of ingredients in a salad - different textures, colors and tastes enliven a salad and make it more interesting - the different emotions we experience simultaneously enliven and enrich our lives.

On the facing page . . .

Under some or all of the salad ingredients write the emotions you are feeling now.

After completing the activity . . .

Journal when you recently felt two or more emotions at a time?

_____

_____

_____

_____

_____

_____

_____

_____

_____

_____

_____

_____

_____

© 2010 WHOLE PERSON ASSOCIATES, 101 W. 2ND ST., SUITE 203, DULUTH MN 55802 • 800-247-6789

The Emotions Salad Bowl

Mourning can be difficult because we feel many emotions at once.

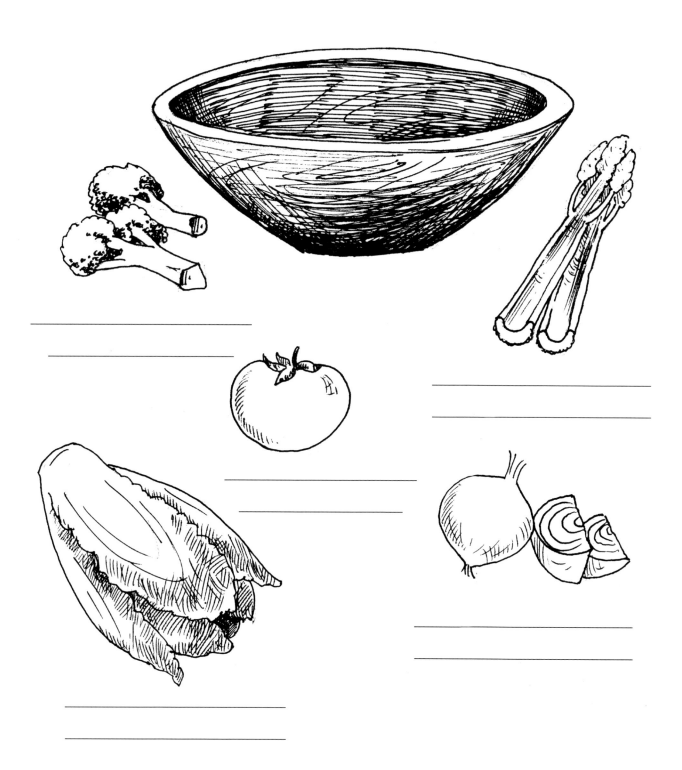

Having many different emotions at the same time adds to the richness of our lives and makes for a much more interesting salad!

About . . .

Serenity Prayer

The *Serenity Prayer*, popularized and adopted by the recovery community, has great validity for all of us. This prayer has become closely associated with 12-step programs, offering strength and calm in pursuit of a more stable life.

On the facing page . . .

recognize the differences between the categories – the things you cannot change (what you have no control over) and the things you can change (what you do have control over). This activity will help you to think about these differences.

After completing the activity . . .

Choose one or more quotations and journal your thoughts.

The art of being wise is the art of knowing what to overlook. ~ William James

Without courage, wisdom bears no fruit. ~ Baltasar Gracian

With courage you will dare to take risks, have the strength to be compassionate, and the wisdom to be humble. Courage is the foundation of integrity.
~ Keshavan Nair

_____

_____

_____

_____

_____

_____

_____

_____

_____

_____

_____

Serenity Prayer

Grant me the serenity to

Accept the things I cannot change . . .

_____

_____

_____

_____

Courage to change the things I can . . .

_____

_____

_____

_____

And the wisdom to know the difference.

About . . .
Control

It is important to realize the limits of what you can control. Remember, we have control only over our own responses and reactions.

On the facing page . . .

List what you can control and what you cannot.

After completing the activity . . .

Journal your thoughts on this quotation by A. J. Kitt

You have no control over what the other guy does.
You only have control over what you do.

_____

_____

_____

_____

_____

_____

_____

_____

_____

_____

_____

_____

_____

_____

Control

THINGS I CAN CONTROL
example: my attitude

_____
_____
_____
_____
_____
_____
_____
_____
_____
_____
_____
_____
_____
_____
_____
_____
_____
_____
_____
_____
_____
_____

THINGS I CANNOT CONTROL
example: the loss

_____
_____
_____
_____
_____
_____
_____
_____
_____
_____
_____
_____
_____
_____
_____
_____
_____
_____
_____
_____
_____
_____

About . . .

FEAR

Many people are reluctant to realize that they are fearful, and even when they can or do admit this to themselves, they are not able to identify what the fears are about. We often recognize that we are angry, anxious or even depressed, but are unaware that fear may be at the root of those feelings. People who experience any type of loss may wonder – how does this affect my life and how will I cope?

Fear of managing life without a loved one is paramount. For many people there is the fear of learning to manage the responsibilities the other person used to do, or coping with the inevitable loneliness that accompanies loss. The first step is to identify what is so frightening. Giving voice to these and other fears is helpful in dealing with a challenge and acknowledging that there is a challenge. It is after getting in touch with these difficult feelings that you can begin to work through them.

On the facing page . . .

Face your fears by sitting quietly, allowing time and emotional space to help you recognize them. It may be helpful to re-phrase the word "fear" to "something that I'm afraid of" or "something that scares me." Then explore three of your fears by responding to the questions.

After completing the activity . . .

C.S. Lewis said, "*No one ever told me that grief felt so much like fear.*"

 What are your thoughts?

_____

_____

_____

_____

_____

_____

_____

_____

FEAR

Fear is a normal response to loss – fear of the unknown, fear of the unfamiliar and fear of the changes in your life.

What do you fear? _____

_____

What are you avoiding because of this fear? _____

_____

What else may be adding to this fear? _____

_____

What steps could you take to work through this fear? _____

_____

- -

What do you fear? _____

_____

What are you avoiding because of this fear? _____

_____

What else may be adding to this fear? _____

_____

What steps could you take to work through this fear? _____

_____

- -

What do you fear? _____

_____

What are you avoiding because of this fear? _____

_____

What else may be adding to this fear? _____

_____

What steps could you take to work through this fear? _____

_____

About . . .
The Guilts

Guilt can be debilitating – therefore it needs to be put in perspective. If the guilt you feel is realistic and reasonable, then the goal would be to learn from it and forgive yourself. Sometimes guilty feelings are unreasonable, born out of unrealistic expectations. It is important to recognize the guilt, acknowledge it, honor it and learn to let it go, or to manage it. Not everyone feels guilt.

On the facing page . . .

After you have identified a recent loss, finish the sentence-starters that apply to you and this loss. You may want to change some of the words in these sentence-starters to words like regret, or feel sorry, badly or lousy.

After completing the activity . . .

Select one or more of the following quotations and journal your thoughts.

The worst guilt is to accept an unearned guilt. ~ Ayn Rand

Guilt is perhaps the most painful companion of death. ~ Coco Chanel

Guilt is anger directed at ourselves – at what we did or did not do.
Resentment is anger directed at others – at what they did or did not do.
~ Peter McWilliams

_____

_____

_____

_____

_____

_____

_____

_____

_____

_____

The Guilts

We all experience losses in our life, and it is common to have feelings of guilt and regret.

Identify a recent loss: _____

I'm sorry I _____ .

I knew _____ .

We didn't talk about _____ .

I wish _____ .

I never should have _____ .

If only I _____ .

How could I have _____ .

Why didn't _____ .

I wish I had _____ .

I am angry _____ .

I did not honor the request that _____ .

I still get upset about _____ .

When I think back I _____ .

About . . .
You're Not Alone

Everyone experiences grief in different ways; however there are many common symptoms. Some symptoms are physical while others are more emotional or spiritual. Whatever you experience is real for you and needs to be accepted and validated. This activity will help you recognize some of the common symptoms of grief. Use it to help you assess your progress along THE HEALING PATHWAY (page 27) by noting your symptoms and how they relate to the various phases.

On the facing page . . .

Check the boxes in the first group that you recognize, fill in additional grief symptoms and where you are right now on THE HEALING PATHWAY.

After completing the activity . . .

Journal the grief symptoms you are experiencing that are most frustrating to you, and explain why.

_____

_____

_____

_____

_____

_____

_____

_____

_____

_____

_____

_____

_____

You're Not Alone

It is comforting to know that grief symptoms happen to everyone.

Which do you recognize?

❑ I am unable to concentrate

❑ I don't want to go anywhere

❑ I feel angry and/or irritable

❑ Nothing interests me

❑ I am upset that the world goes on as normal

❑ I hear a familiar song and cry

❑ I feel like I am losing my mind

❑ I do not want to get out of bed in the morning

Additional grief symptoms that happen to me:

❑ _____

❑ _____

❑ _____

❑ _____

❑ _____

❑ _____

❑ _____

❑ _____

Where do you think you are right now on THE HEALING PATHWAY? *(page 29)*

❑ Shock

❑ Disorganization

❑ Reorganization

What to do with my memories?

Memories of loved ones and shared times are very important. It is sometimes confusing because often memories provoke strong feelings, sometimes feelings of sadness because of missing the person and sometimes feelings of relief because of no longer needing to deal with some unpleasant aspect of the person or situation or because the person is no longer suffering. When something is remembered, smiles or tears may come, depending on what is evoked. The wide range of these emotions is to be expected. Remember, it is important to feel what you feel and then move on.

On the facing page . . .

One way to do this is to treasure memories (even the unpleasant ones), share them with trusted others, or journal about them. Notice the feeling and stay with it without judging; sit quietly and feel what you are feeling about a particular memory. When you stay with the feeling you will often notice how the feelings shift. You may also notice physical sensations, i.e., tightness in the chest, breath changes, etc. As these are happening, make a decision as to what to do with this particular memory – put it in your memory book and savor it, or, perhaps put it aside and come back to it another time.

Examples:

KEEP AND SAVOR	MEMENTO BOX
Love letters	Looking at photographs
Baseball card collection	Rereading the condolence letters
Toys	Baby shoes

After completing the activity . . .

What is a memory that you love to think about and why?

_____

_____

_____

_____

_____

_____

What to do with my memories?

Memories to keep and to savor	Memories to put aside and return to later
	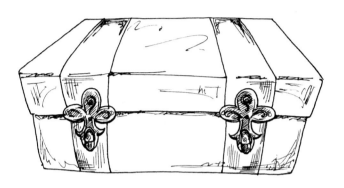

_____	_____
_____	_____
_____	_____
_____	_____
_____	_____
_____	_____
_____	_____
_____	_____
_____	_____
_____	_____
_____	_____

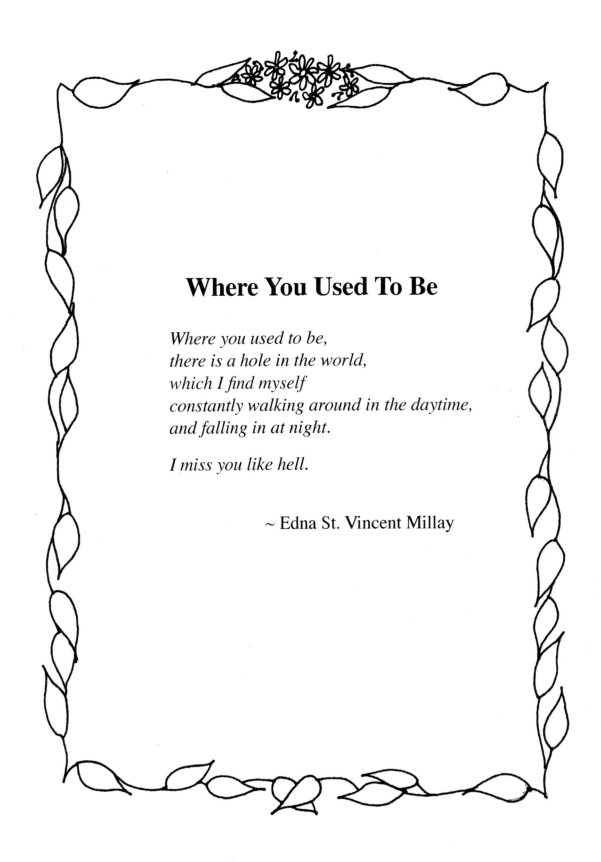

Where You Used To Be

Where you used to be,
there is a hole in the world,
which I find myself
constantly walking around in the daytime,
and falling in at night.

I miss you like hell.

~ Edna St. Vincent Millay

CHAPTER 3

Telling Your Story

The value of giving people who are grieving the opportunity to share their stories cannot be overstated. It is extremely important for people to process their experiences by talking about them. Journaling is another way of "talking" and at this point, it may be wise to purchase a journal, if you haven't already done so. Some people will have a need to retell details of their loved one's dying process; others may need to share details of an illness, or various aspects of the person's life.

About . . .

Memento Activity

It is very important for you to talk or journal about your loved one and the circumstances of the loss, as well as to focus on accomplishments, attributes and/or shared activities.

On the facing page . . .

Take a look at the illustrations for some memento suggestions. Other possibilities are books, examples from hobbies, gifts, knick-knacks, cards, poems, etc.

After looking over the illustrations and choosing a momento . . .

Use your memento as a prop and journal about the memory it brings to mind, the relationship you shared with your loved one and/or the attributes that had a strong impact on you.

_____

_____

_____

_____

_____

_____

_____

_____

_____

_____

_____

_____

_____

Memento Activity

About . . .
THE DAY WE MET

It is helpful for you to remember past experiences. Looking back in time provides the opportunity to focus on memories. This may provoke a sadness regarding what was lost, however, remembering your history can be quite healing.

On the facing page . . .

Journal about the day you met your loved one.

Example:

"The day we met _____" can start out like:

- *My son was born at 10:36 p.m. on April 9, 1956, weighing 9# 6½ ounces. What a cutie!*

- *My mom brought home a man she was dating when I was eight. I was afraid of him.*

- *I was on a beach and a two-legged mermaid appeared in an orange bikini!*

After journaling on the facing page . . .

you can continue your thoughts here.

_____

_____

_____

_____

_____

_____

_____

_____

_____

THE DAY WE MET

_____

_____

_____

_____

_____

_____

_____

_____

_____

_____

_____

_____

About . . .

Part of My Story Is . . .

A journaling activity often helps people sort through memories and feelings. This page will inspire both.

On the facing page . . .

Complete the sentence starters.

After completing the activity . . .

Feel free to expand upon any of the sentence starters on the facing page.

_____

_____

_____

_____

_____

_____

_____

_____

_____

_____

_____

_____

_____

_____

_____

_____

Part of My Story Is . . .

I am sad when _____

I am angry about _____

I miss _____

I wish _____

Time with family now is _____

I would like to have told my loved one _____

I cry when _____

Being alone feels _____

I've discovered _____

It's just too much when _____

I get upset when _____

My friends _____

I hate when _____

I am grateful for _____

I am surprised that _____

I treasure _____

It's helpful when _____

I have learned that _____

It's difficult for me when _____

My family _____

About

When My Loved One Died

It is important for you to have the opportunity to tell the story of your loved one's death, and your feelings at the time, as often as you need. Most people who are grieving benefit by talking about what happened as well as their individual relationship with that person or event. However, often well-meaning friends and family members get tired of hearing the story repeated. Journaling and/or participating in a grief support group are ways to sort through your memories and feelings.

On the facing page . . .

Complete the sentence starters.

After completing the activity . . .

Continue to journal by expanding upon any of the sentence starters.

_____

_____

_____

_____

_____

_____

_____

_____

_____

_____

_____

_____

_____

_____

When My Loved One Died

I was _____

_____ .

The week before _____

_____ .

That day _____

_____ .

The day after _____

_____ .

The funeral or memorial service _____

_____ .

The family _____

_____ .

My friends _____

_____ .

The most difficult part was _____

_____ .

I was surprised _____

_____ .

I was angry _____

_____ .

I hadn't expected _____

_____ .

Action is the antidote to despair.

~ Joan Baez

CHAPTER 4

Self-Care

When people are mourning, it is quite common for them to neglect themselves. This is exacerbated when they have been caretakers. The goal of this chapter is to help you recognize the need to take care of yourself in all five domains:

- Physical
- Intellectual
- Emotional
- Social
- Spiritual

About . . .

Self-Care Domains

There are five areas (domains) of life: physical (body), intellectual (mind), emotional (psychological), social (relationships) and spiritual (inner self). It is important to understand the need to take care of yourself in all five domains.

On the facing page . . .

The pie chart illustrates that each domain is of equal importance and needs attention. Most people tend to do a reasonable job of taking care of themselves in a few areas while neglecting others. In each domain, list the activities you are doing to take care of yourself.

Many activities will fall into more than one domain.

> An example of an activity that has many benefits for some people is **walking**:
>
> > *Physical* – because of health benefits
> >
> > *Spiritual* – because I walk in nature
> >
> > *Emotional* – because walking is a stress-buster for me
> >
> > *Social* – because I do it with a friend

After completing the activity . . .

Record what you do for yourself over the course of a week, noting the self-care activity in the appropriate piece of the pie. Journal about the benefits you derive from the various activities and which domains need more attention.

_____

_____

_____

_____

_____

_____

_____

_____

_____

Self-Care Domains

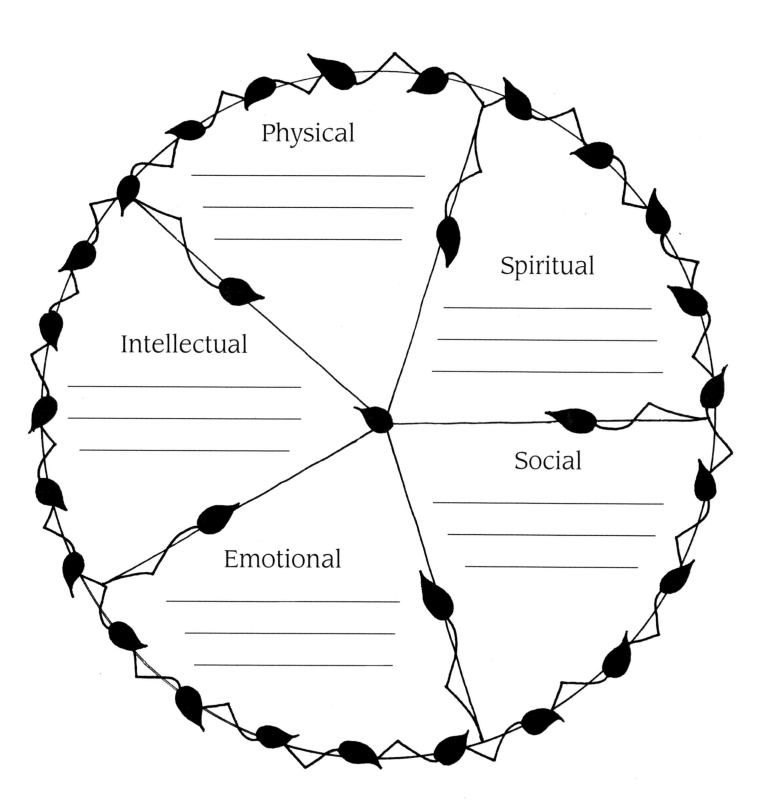

Physical

_____

_____

_____

Spiritual

_____

_____

_____

Intellectual

_____

_____

_____

Social

_____

_____

_____

Emotional

_____

_____

_____

About . . .
Are You Taking Care of Yourself?

This self-assessment tool can be used to help you determine what you are doing to take care of yourself and what you are willing to try.

On the facing page . . .

Review the grid and check the appropriate boxes.

After completing the activity . . .

Think and journal about the importance of the items on the list, how you manage the things you have always done, and how you can manage those you are willing to do.

_____

_____

_____

_____

_____

_____

_____

_____

_____

_____

_____

_____

_____

_____

_____

_____

Are You Taking Care of Yourself?

		Yes, I'm doing it!	No, not yet	This is not for me!
1	Are you eating three healthy meals a day?			
2	Do you belong to a support group or social group that meets at least once a month?			
3	Do you do something to relax at least three times a day?			
4	Are you keeping your mind stimulated?			
5	Do you exercise at least three times a week?			
6	Are you keeping your appointments and obligations?			
7	Do you sleep six to eight hours each night?			
8	Are you kind to yourself?			
9	Do you take your medicines as prescribed?			
10	Do you say NO when you need/want to?			
11	Are you forgiving yourself?			
12	Do you enjoy poetry and/or spiritual readings?			
13	Are you engaged in social activities?			
14	Are you journaling?			
15	Are you balancing between "being" (feeling your feelings) and "doing" (keeping busy)?			

About . . .
Counting My Blessings

Focusing on the positive aspects of life is extremely beneficial. It is important to identify and appreciate your blessings and be grateful.

This can be used for "big" blessings like family, community, good health, safety, or a Higher Power, or for the "little" blessings one has during the course of the day like seeing a beautiful flower, hearing a bird chirp or feeling the warmth of the sun shining.

On the facing page . . .

List some of your blessings in the stars.

On a separate sheet of paper, write a minimum of three blessings at the end of each day.

After completing the activity . . .

Post your blessings in obvious places, where you can be reminded of the blessings in your life (your mirror, refrigerator, car, workplace, etc.).

Journal your thoughts about this quotation by Maltbie D. Babcock, and how it applies to you.

> *Better to lose count while naming your blessings than to lose your blessings while counting your troubles.*

_____

_____

_____

_____

_____

_____

_____

_____

_____

_____

Counting My Blessings

At certain times in our lives it is so easy to focus on the negatives and overlook what we have to be grateful for.

Remind yourself every day of how truly blessed you are.

About . . .

Ways to Nourish Myself

It is worthwhile to recognize the various ways you already take care of yourself, and to be open and consider adding other self-nurturing behaviors.

On the facing page . . .

Check off those *self-nourishments* that are already part of your life, and in the blank spaces, add things you do that are not on the list. With another color pen, check the things that you are willing to try in the next month, again adding items in the blanks.

After completing the activity . . .

Journal about some of the *self-nourishing* things you did in the past that you no longer do, and the obstacles to returning to those previous activities.

_____

_____

_____

_____

_____

_____

_____

_____

_____

_____

_____

_____

_____

_____

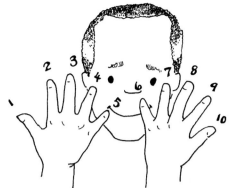

Ways to Nourish Myself
Let the healing begin!

- ❏ get involved in something new
- ❏ write in a journal
- ❏ call a friend
- ❏ take a long warm bath & light a candle
- ❏ listen to music
- ❏ read
- ❏ work in a garden
- ❏ go for a hike
- ❏ _____
- ❏ _____
- ❏ _____
- ❏ _____
- ❏ _____
- ❏ _____
- ❏ _____

- ❏ start a craft or hobby
- ❏ exercise
- ❏ meditate
- ❏ attend a place of worship
- ❏ go to a movie, even if I cry
- ❏ visit a museum
- ❏ care for a pet or plant
- ❏ volunteer_____
- ❏ _____
- ❏ _____
- ❏ _____
- ❏ _____
- ❏ _____
- ❏ _____

About . . .
There is a fine line

Paying attention to what you are doing, and the reasons for doing it is important. For example, accepting social invitations can be beneficial in preventing isolation, and it may be useful to accept every invitation from friends for a while. However, you need to know when too much is simply too much. Sometimes it may be important to decline an invitation so you have time to yourself. Likewise praying or meditating is an "alone" activity that can bring great comfort to some people. Spending all your time in prayer or meditation is not wise. It is essential to find a balance between busy-ness and still-ness.

On the facing page . . .

In the first column, list what you are doing to keep busy. In the second column, list what you are doing to make time for yourself to heal.

After completing the activity. . .

Journal your thoughts about this quotation from Alan D. Wolfelt, Ph.D.

As I experience my grief, I'm pulled to be both alone and together with others. I realize I need both. The beauty of it is that I have discovered I can embrace both needs. One does not preclude the other. What an important revelation!

_____

_____

_____

_____

_____

_____

_____

_____

_____

There is a fine line

between keeping busy after a loss yet not being
too busy to grieve, and ultimately heal.
Finding that balance is the challenge.

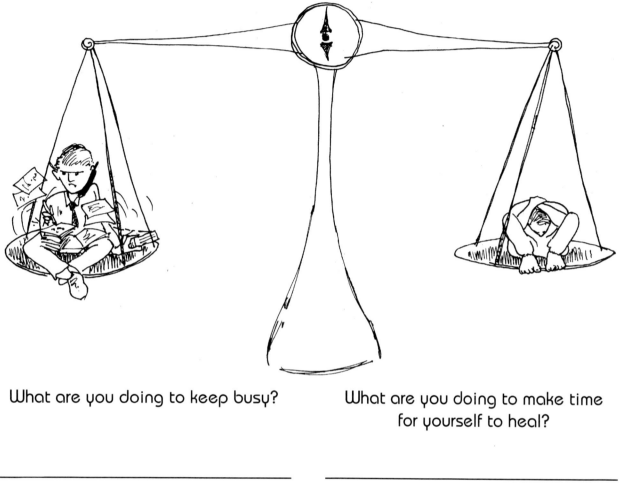

What are you doing to keep busy?

What are you doing to make time
for yourself to heal?

_____

_____

_____

_____

_____

_____

Is this a healthy balance?

About . . .

ORGANIZING IS WHAT IT'S ALL ABOUT!

During the grieving process it is very common to feel overwhelmed. Even the most organized people feel as though they cannot keep track of what they need to do. This activity will help people who are feeling disorganized regain some sense of control.

On the facing page . . .

Listed are some suggestions. Check those that you already do and then, add your own ideas.

After completing the activity . . .

Choose one or more of these quotations and journal your thoughts.

Organizing is what you do before you do something, so that when you do it, it is not all mixed up. ~ A. A. Milne

Successful organizing is based on the recognition that people get organized because they, too, have a vision. ~ Paul Wellstone

The trouble with organizing a thing is that pretty soon folks get to paying more attention to the organization than to what they're organized for.

~ Laura Ingalls Wilder

_____

_____

_____

_____

_____

_____

_____

_____

_____

_____

_____

ORGANIZING IS WHAT IT'S ALL ABOUT!

To do...

Using time wisely and feeling in control of the day helps to de-stress!

Here are some suggestions.

- ❏ Keep an ongoing "TO-DO" list and check items as they are completed.

- ❏ Break down large projects into small manageable tasks and put each one on your TO-DO list.

- ❏ Keep keys, eyeglasses, wallet, etc., in the same place at all times.

- ❏ Set your alarm 15-30 minutes early to give yourself plenty of time.

- ❏ Clean home or apartment one room at a time.

- ❏ Keep only one calendar. Write every appointment on it and refer to it daily.

- ❏ Bring something to do with you when waiting for appointments (balance check book, write TO-DO lists or letters, read a humorous book, knit, etc.).

- ❏ Plan menus once a week and purchase the ingredients at one time, if time is limited. If it's not and you want to keep busy, plan meals in the morning, shop each day and prepare that day.

- ❏ Cluster similar errands together.

- ❏ Keep the cell phone, calendar, and your to-do list in the same place at all times.

- ❏ Delegate assignments to co-workers or family members. It's OK to have others help you and it is a gift to them to be asked to do something.

- ❏ Get rid of clutter. It is a great feeling to look around your home and see it in order. Living with clutter can be energy-draining.

- ❏ Try not to let things pile up. Set aside a time each day to file paperwork, pay bills or sort through the mail to avoid overwhelming and unmanageable piles.

- ❏ Keep frequently used information and files in a place that is easily accessible.

- ❏ _____
- ❏ _____
- ❏ _____
- ❏ _____
- ❏ _____
- ❏ _____
- ❏ _____
- ❏ _____
- ❏ _____
- ❏ _____

About . . .

SO MUCH TO DO

People who are grieving often feel disoriented, disorganized and unable to function as usual. Sometimes people truly believe that they are not doing or accomplishing anything at all. This activity will help you realize that you are getting things done, but are probably taking more time and energy than you would like.

On the facing page . . .

At the end of a day, write what you accomplished that day. (On low-energy days, it is OK to say, "ate breakfast" or "brushed teeth.") Complete the facing activity over the course of a week and then, recognize and celebrate all of the tasks you completed.

After completing the activity . . .

Journal a recent example of how you felt when you were able to accomplish something you needed to, but didn't want to.

_____

_____

_____

_____

_____

_____

_____

_____

_____

_____

_____

_____

_____

_____

_____

So Much To Do
So little energy or inclination!

You might be getting more done than you think!

DAY	ACCOMPLISHMENTS
Monday	
Tuesday	
Wednesday	
Thursday	
Friday	
Saturday	
Sunday	

About . . .

Being the Best You Can Be

Remember to be aware of your own self-care. This is a time in your life when it takes a lot of energy to do almost anything. This often impacts relationships as well as how you feel about yourself.

On the facing page . . .

See the self-care possibilities and write your thoughts next to them.

After completing the activity . . .

Journal what you already do to take care of yourself and what you would like to add. If you feel you are doing a particularly good job in some areas, note that also.

_____

_____

_____

_____

_____

_____

_____

_____

_____

_____

_____

_____

_____

_____

_____

_____

Being the Best You Can Be

Exercise to regain energy. _____

Walk proud with shoulders back and a bounce in your step. _____

_____

Find ways to laugh. _____

Nod and/or smile when passing someone. _____

Find something beautiful about each day and focus on it. _____

_____

Make a list of things to do and cross off each as it is accomplished. _____

_____

Create something. _____

Eat healthy. _____

Make a list of long-term goals. Share them with loved ones. _____

_____

Drink plenty of water and limit caffeine. _____

Take time for yourself. _____

Focus on something for which you are grateful. _____

_____

_____

About . . .
Leisure

Leisure or recreational activities serve many healthful purposes. They can be intellectually stimulating, emotionally fulfilling, promote socialization, and provide physical and/or spiritual outlets. Remember the need for varied activities for a healthy lifestyle, even during the grieving process. This directly relates to *Self-Care Domains*, page 65.

On the facing page . . .

In the second column, list some leisure activities that you can do that will fulfill the goals in the first column.

After completing the activity on the facing page . . .

Journal your obstacles to participating in leisure activities (lack of time, financial concerns, low energy, feeling guilty about having a good time, etc.) and how you have, or can, overcome those obstacles.

_____

_____

_____

_____

_____

_____

_____

_____

_____

_____

_____

_____

_____

_____

Leisure

Participating in leisure activities can make a difference
in the physical, intellectual, emotional, social, and spiritual facets
of your life!

MY GOAL	A LEISURE ACTIVITY I CAN DO
Accomplish something	
Be alone	
Be a spectator	
Be creative	
Be sociable	
Be spiritually uplifted	
Compete	
Continue to learn	
Exercise alone	
Exercise with others	
Help someone else	
Keep emotionally stimulated	
Keep mentally stimulated	
Keep physically stimulated	
Play	
Relax	
Return to my hobby	
Spend time with family	

About . . .

A Sacred Space

Creating a special place for quiet, prayer, meditation or reminiscing can be healing. A sacred space is a place for you and your thoughts. It need not take up much room, but it should be a place where you can be alone, quiet and comfortable. Some people want mementos of their loved one in the space (a shrine of sorts) and others want a soothing space without mementos at all.

On the facing page . . .

Answer the questions posed, imagining that you are creating a sacred space.

After completing the activity . . .

How can you create such a space and designate time to spend in it?

_____

_____

_____

_____

_____

_____

_____

_____

_____

_____

_____

_____

_____

_____

_____

_____

A Sacred Space

A sacred space promotes a sense of healing. It might be helpful to create a sacred place.

Where can you find a safe and sacred place? _____

_____

What color would be most soothing? _____

_____

What objects would you keep in this space? _____

_____

What aroma would be pleasing? _____

_____

What music would be comforting? _____

_____

What mementos would you bring into this space? _____

_____

What else would make this space sacred? _____

_____

Whom would you trust to see this space? _____

_____

About . . .

My Prayer Today

Prayer can provide an opportunity to tap into your spirituality. It is a way to communicate with the universe, spirits, higher power, God – or whatever moves your soul. It can be useful to journal, to let loose and pray in any way, with any words that you need. You may be angry and yell, petition or ask for guidance, give thanks for your blessings or you just may want to pour your heart out.

On the facing page . . .

Create your own prayer.

After completing the activity . . .

Reflect on this prayer by David Feldt:

> **Source of Healing**
> *Spread over me*
> *the shelter of your peace,*
> *that I might reside there,*
> *through this journey*
> *of sadness and pain*
> *that I might some day*
> *find the strength to return*
> *to life and its blessings.*

Abraham Joshua Heschel says, *In the act of prayer . . . we restore our mental health.*

Journal your reaction to either the prayer or the quotation.

_____

_____

_____

_____

_____

_____

_____

_____

My Prayer Today

About . . .

Need a Good Cry?

Crying is a good thing – for men and women – emotionally and physiologically. Like laughter, crying releases tension and can help your body repair. Crying can be beneficial in terms of releasing hormones and pent up feelings. For some people it is difficult to cry. If you are unable to cry, that is okay. It is not imperative that you cry.

On the facing page . . .

If you feel blocked and want to cry but have been unable to, you may find the suggestions useful, and perhaps you can add your own.

After completing the activity . . .

Read the following words of Washington Irving.

There is a sacredness in tears. They are not the mark of weakness, but of power. They speak more eloquently than ten thousand tongues. They are messengers of overwhelming grief . . . and unspeakable love.

Journal about a time when you unexpectedly started to cry. How did you feel afterwards (relieved, embarrassed, tired, relaxed, etc.).

_____

_____

_____

_____

_____

_____

_____

_____

_____

_____

_____

Need a Good Cry?

Crying helps to get the sad out of you!

Watch a tear-jerking movie.

Listen to music.

Look at photographs.

Talk with people who share your loss.

Hold a special memento and focus on the memory it evokes.

_____

_____

_____

_____

_____

_____

_____

_____

_____

_____

About . . .

It Helps to Smile

So many people believe that it is not appropriate, or respectful to the deceased, to smile, laugh or enjoy oneself after a loss. It is not only okay to have a good time but it is beneficial to healing. Laughter and humor have healing properties. They make you feel better and also help others feel more comfortable being with you.

On the facing page . . .

Check the suggestions that you would be willing to try in the next month.

After completing the activity . . .

Read the following quotations, choose one or both and journal your reactions.

Birds sing after a storm; why shouldn't people feel as free to delight in whatever remains to them.

~ Rose Fitzgerald Kennedy

Don't cry because it's over, smile because it happened.

~ Dr. Seuss – Theodor Seuss Geisel

_____

_____

_____

_____

_____

_____

_____

_____

_____

_____

_____

_____

It Helps to Smile

but it's not always so easy after a loss. However, humor and laughter are essential to well-being!

- ❑ Share funny, clever emails.
- ❑ Watch funny, even silly, sitcoms.

  (*some favorites:*_____)
- ❑ Rent humorous movies.

  (*some favorites:*_____)
- ❑ Sing a fun song or commercial.

  (*some favorites:*_____)
- ❑ Watch humorous talk shows on television.

  (*some favorites:*_____)
- ❑ Go to the movies, but check first to be sure it's funny.

  (*some favorites:*_____)
- ❑ Play board games or cards.

  (*some favorites:*_____)
- ❑ Play with a baby.
- ❑ Share funny memories.

Other ways to keep smiling:

- ❑ _____
- ❑ _____
- ❑ _____
- ❑ _____
- ❑ _____
- ❑ _____
- ❑ _____
- ❑ _____
- ❑ _____
- ❑ _____

About . . .
SELF-TALK

Self-talk is internal dialogue - the words we use when we talk to ourselves. Our self-talk often reflects and creates our emotional state. It can influence our self-esteem, outlook, energy level, performance and relationships. It can even affect our health, determining, for example, how we handle stressful events.

Most people have a self-critical voice that talks almost non-stop. This negative self-talk can be replaced by positive self-talk. The things you say to yourself, silently or aloud, have great influence on your mood, energy, self-esteem and attitude. The words you use and their messages, have power, influencing how you interpret the world and your emotional state.

On the facing page . . .

Read the negative self-talk examples in the left column and fill in the corresponding box with positive self-talk.

After completing the activity . . .

Journal some of the phrases you are aware of saying to yourself and when you say them.

How has this self-talk impacted you?

_____

_____

_____

_____

_____

_____

_____

_____

_____

_____

_____

SELF-TALK

Let's work on positive self-talk.

MY NEGATIVE SELF-TALK	MY POSITIVE SELF-TALK
I am forgetting everything – I hate it!	*It is OK to forget. I'm not forgetting <u>everything</u>!*
I do everything wrong.	*I do some things wrong. That means I do <u>some</u> things right!*
I am so unsure of myself right now.	
I need to be on time and never late.	
I will not ask for help. It shows I'm incompetent.	
I cannot do the things I used to do.	
I am so tense all the time.	
It shows weakness if I cry.	
I feel so anxious I can hardly breathe.	
I SHOULD say "yes" to every invitation.	
I will never ever get over it.	
I cannot handle this.	
This is impossible.	
I could have done better.	

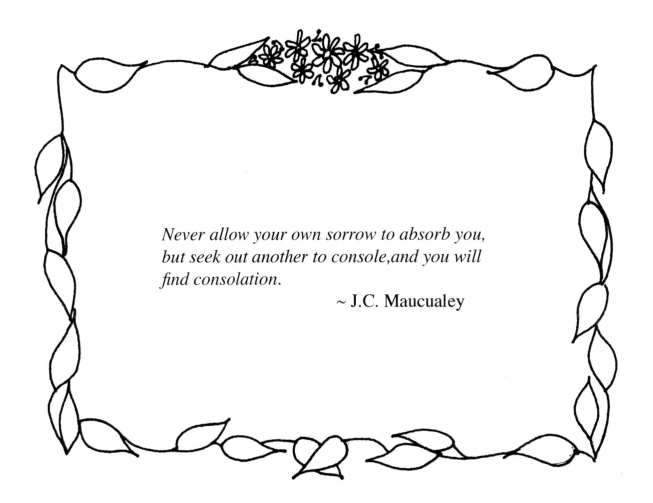

Never allow your own sorrow to absorb you,
but seek out another to console, and you will
find consolation.

~ J.C. Maucualey

CHAPTER 5

Relationships

Many people who are grieving experience changes in their relationships. There are people in our lives who are supportive; they somehow know just what to say or do. Others want to be helpful, but simply do not know what to say or do. Others seem to disappear. This secondary loss can increase a sense of isolation and loneliness.

The pages in this chapter offer an opportunity for you to realistically look at the changes in your relationships. These activities will help you realize that supportive people in your life often need to be given specific tasks. Can you ask for help? The activities are designed to encourage asking for help and appreciating those who are providing support.

About . . .
MY SUPPORT NETWORK

Often people who are grieving feel lonely and isolated. This page will remind you that you have supportive people in your life. Remember, just as one person may fill more than one role, seldom does one person meet all of your needs.

On the facing page . . .

In the second column fill in the names of the people who fit the roles listed in the first column. You can duplicate the names if they fill multiple roles and you can list several names for a single role in the second column. Leave blank those roles that do not apply. If you have other roles not listed, fill them in at the bottom.

After completing the activity . . .

Read this quotation by Rona Barrett and journal your thoughts.

The healthy and strong individual is the one who asks for help when he needs it, whether he has an abscess on his knee or in his soul.

_____

_____

_____

_____

_____

_____

_____

_____

_____

_____

_____

_____

_____

MY SUPPORT NETWORK

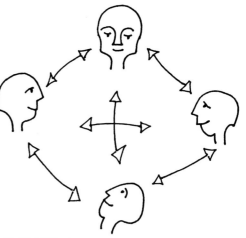

One supportive person does not usually meet every one of our needs.

ROLE	Who can I turn to for this role?
Share problems	
Talk about the loss	
Give good advice	
Energize me	
Have a fun time	
Accept me as I am	
Try something adventuresome	
Keep me busy / distracted	
Provide reassurance	
Relax with me	
Meditate with me	
Enjoy a good laugh	
Appreciate the outdoors and nature	
Discuss family issues	
Take a walk	
Go shopping	
Study	
Tell me the truth even if I don't like it	
Work with	
Have lunch with	
Disagree with me when necessary	
Share my spiritual life	
Help with chores	

About. . .

Support System

Some needs are met by more than one relationship and seldom does one single relationship meet all of your needs. This activity will help you sort out the members of your support team and how they can be helpful.

On the facing page . . .

Name one or more people in each category and write the need they fill for you. Skip those that do not pertain to you.

After completing the activity . . .

To whom can you turn when you're feeling lonely? Why that person?

_____

_____

_____

_____

_____

_____

_____

_____

Who is another supportive person in your life? Journal more about that person and what makes him or her so supportive.

_____

_____

_____

_____

_____

_____

_____

_____

Support System

Seldom does one relationship meet all of your needs.

CATEGORY	NAME	NEED BEING FILLED
Parent		
Grandparent		
Sibling		
Child		
Significant other		
Good Friend		
Neighbor		
Counselor		
Clergy		
Club		
Co-worker/Boss		
Support Group		
Pet		

RELATIONSHIPS CHANGE

Throughout life, relationships change – nothing is static. After a loss, your sensitivities to these changes may be heightened. It is natural to focus on the major relationship change you have experienced – the loss of your loved one. This activity will help you become more aware of some of the other relationships in your life. Notice if they have changed. If so, in what way? Be aware and accept the movement or shifts that are a part of all relationships. Compare the relationship prior to your loss, to this present time – not years and years ago, and not in your idealized version.

On the facing page . . .

Write the name of a family member, friend, neighbor, or acquaintance in each circle.

Put a **+** if it is a positive change

Put a **–** if it's a negative change

Put an **S** for the same.

After completing the activity . . .

Think of relationships you had as a child – maybe a best friend or a beloved teacher. How did that relationship change and shift over time?

_____

_____

_____

_____

Journal about people from whom you can and should (for your own healing) distance yourself for the time being. Are there other strategies you might use to deal with uncomfortable changes?

_____

_____

_____

_____

RELATIONSHIPS CHANGE

How have your relationships changed since the loss?

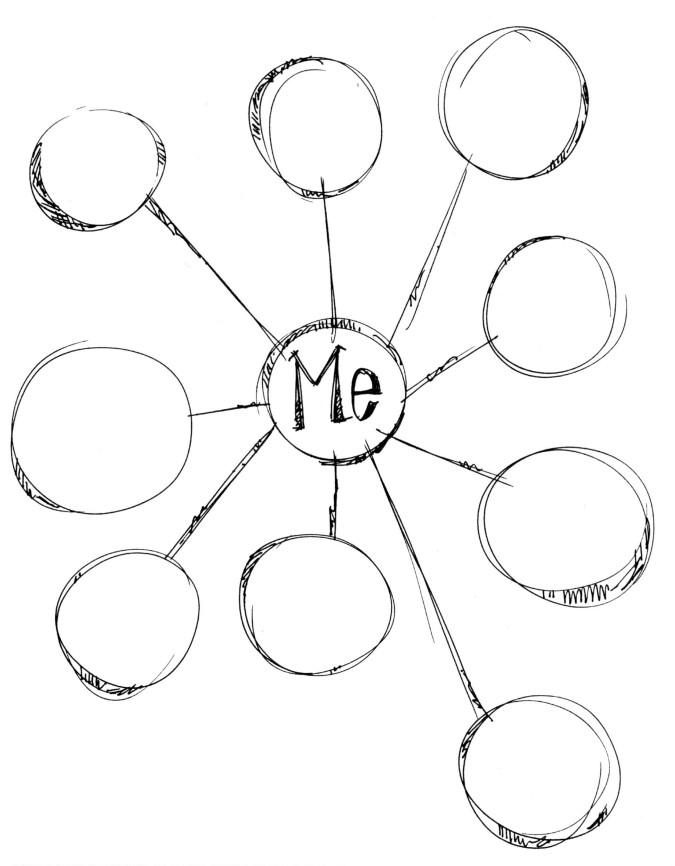

About . . .
Supportive Friends

Throughout life, our needs are in constant motion. Friendships shift with changing life circumstances. It may be that this is a time when you need more support and encouragement than you have needed in the past. This activity will help you look at your friendships, see how they are meeting your current needs and help you figure out what you want in a friend right now.

On the facing page . . .

In each section, name one friend and check the boxes that apply to that particular friendship.

After completing the activity . . .

Read this quotation from William James and journal whether it is true in your life.

> *Great emergencies and crisis show us how much greater our vital resources are than we had supposed.*

_____

_____

_____

_____

_____

_____

_____

_____

_____

_____

_____

_____

_____

Supportive Friends

What do you need in a friend right now?

- -

Name a good friend. _____

Check off if this is true of this friendship:

- ❑ Open communication
- ❑ Acceptance of each other
- ❑ Fun to be with
- ❑ Do not fix or control the other
- ❑ Listen to each other
- ❑ _____

- ❑ Clear boundaries
- ❑ Trust each other
- ❑ OK to have other friendships
- ❑ Give and receive
- ❑ Open to feedback
- ❑ _____

Comments _____

- -

Name a good friend. _____

Check off if this is true of this friendship:

- ❑ Open communication
- ❑ Acceptance of each other
- ❑ Fun to be with
- ❑ Do not fix or control the other
- ❑ Listen to each other
- ❑ _____

- ❑ Clear boundaries
- ❑ Trust each other
- ❑ OK to have other friendships
- ❑ Give and receive
- ❑ Open to feedback
- ❑ _____

Comments _____

- -

Name a good friend. _____

Check off if this is true of this friendship:

- ❑ Open communication
- ❑ Acceptance of each other
- ❑ Fun to be with
- ❑ Do not fix or control the other
- ❑ Listen to each other
- ❑ _____

- ❑ Clear boundaries
- ❑ Trust each other
- ❑ OK to have other friendships
- ❑ Give and receive
- ❑ Open to feedback
- ❑ _____

Comments _____

Asking for Help

Many people who are grieving do not know how to ask for help and yet feel quite overwhelmed with the tasks at hand. So often, friends and family members want to be helpful but cannot think of concrete things to offer. They may say things like "Call me if you need anything" or "What can I do?" Without thinking about it in advance, offers like that get under-utilized.

You may have people in your life who would be happy to help, but may not know what, or how, to offer. It is a real gift to a friend and/or family member to make a concrete request. When asking for help, you might tell the person to whom you are making the request, that you expect them to say "no" if they need or want to. Friendships can flourish when both the giver and receiver are honest. It is valuable to create opportunities for friends and family members to help. This often creates a healing atmosphere.

On the facing page . . .

Write the names of people you would trust to help you with some of the items listed.

After completing the activity . . .

Journal how you feel when you help someone. Can you give an example?

_____

_____

_____

_____

_____

_____

_____

_____

_____

_____

_____

Asking for Help

How can you allow people to help you?

Accompany me to a . . .

lawyer _____

physician _____

accountant _____

financial advisor _____

store _____

movie, museum, concert, etc. _____

other _____

Make phone calls to the . . .

professional advisor(s) _____

bank/credit union _____

Social Security office _____

child's school _____

other _____

Help with children by . . .

baby sitting _____

taking to movie, shopping, library, park, museum _____

reading _____

driving/car pool _____

other _____

Help with these chores . . .

shop _____

walk the dog _____

car wash, gas, service _____

pick up dry cleaning, help with laundry _____

meals _____

yard work _____

water plants _____

other _____

Correspondence _____

House or pet sit _____

Listen _____

About . . .
They Mean Well

Often well-meaning people say things that upset us. They mean well, but may not know what to say, or how to say what they mean, or may say things they believe will be helpful, but yet, what they say is not comforting. They may not even know of your loss. People sometimes think they are complimenting us, but it may feel more like pressure ("You're being so strong.") You will probably continue to hear those sorts of comments. Some may be upsetting and others may not. Sometimes we are stunned by a comment and don't know how to respond.

This activity provides an opportunity to plan and rehearse how to respond if you continue to receive upsetting comments. Sometimes saying nothing is perfectly fine.

On the facing page . . .

Check any of the statements that were said to you and that upset you. In the next section, add your own. In the last section, create some appropriate responses.

After completing the activity . . .

Do you recognize the clichés in these poems by Pearl Joseph?

Cold Comfort

It's all for the best
At least he didn't suffer
Time heals all wounds
I know just how you feel
Time will heal

There's no sense dwelling on the past
God never gives us more than we can handle
You're fortunate; you had many wonderful
    years together
Life goes on

Everything happens for a reason
If you look around, others are worse off than you
You should be over this by now
Count your blessings

Cold Comfort – for Parents

God needed him as an angel in heaven
He's better off now
He's in a better place
Only the good die young

At least you have other children
Your other children must be such a
    consolation for you
Don't cry, be strong for the children
It's God's will

Think of a time you said something insensitive and wished you could have taken your words back. Journal about it.

_____

_____

_____

They Mean Well

People mean well and want to help, but the things they say are sometimes not helpful.

Check any of these that were said to you:

- ❑ How are you doing?
- ❑ It's probably for the best.
- ❑ Don't take it so hard.
- ❑ Why didn't you call me?
- ❑ I know how you feel.
- ❑ It was God's will.
- ❑ Don't cry.
- ❑ You must be relieved.
- ❑ You're so strong.
- ❑ You're lucky to have had her or him for so long.
- ❑ It will be all right.
- ❑ How is _____(the name of the deceased)?

What other things have been said to you?

- ❑ _____
- ❑ _____
- ❑ _____
- ❑ _____
- ❑ _____
- ❑ _____
- ❑ _____
- ❑ _____
- ❑ _____
- ❑ _____
- ❑ _____
- ❑ _____
- ❑ _____
- ❑ _____

Select several from the list above that are similar to what has been said to you and write how you could respond if it is said to you in the future.

- ❑ How are you doing?   (EXAMPLE) *I'm having a difficult day. Thanks for asking.*
- ❑ _____
- ❑ _____
- ❑ _____

About . . .

Why Do Friends Drop Away?

Many people experience the secondary loss of friends who no longer reach out to them after a loved one dies. It is helpful for you to understand that this phenomenon is not unique to you. Although it may be difficult, sometimes it is important for you to reach out to your friends. Some ways to maintain contact are:

Call people you haven't heard from

Make plans and invite someone to join you

Return phone calls

Send an email

Send a greeting card

On the facing page . . .

Put a check mark by any of the statements that might apply to you and your friends, and add your own at the bottom.

After completing the activity . . .

Think of a time you were friends with someone who suffered a loss. In what ways were you attentive to that friend? As you reflect on that experience, is there something you wish you had done differently?

_____

_____

_____

_____

_____

_____

_____

_____

_____

_____

Why Do Friends Drop Away?

❑ They may be frustrated because they cannot help me feel better.

❑ We now have different lifestyles.

❑ They want to find me someone new, and I am not ready.

❑ They have never had a loss like mine and cannot understand my grief.

❑ They want me to be done grieving. I'm not.

❑ They are uncomfortable with their own feelings, let alone mine.

❑ It is difficult for them to see me without the person I lost.

❑ They are afraid that something might happen to them or to someone close.

❑ I am not as cheerful as they would like, and they do not want to be pulled down.

❑ I am a reminder of the loss.

❑ They are tired of hearing my story, but I still need to tell it.

❑ I don't fit in with their social group anymore.

❑ They called me often, but I didn't call them.

❑ Maybe they didn't invite me because they assumed I would be uncomfortable. I might need to initiate.

❑ I wanted so much to tell my story. I might have forgotten to listen to others' stories.

❑ In every conversation, I think I interject something about my loss. That might get tiresome.

❑ They are concerned that I might be a threat to their marriage.

❑ I am needier than I used to be.

❑ I have more time on my hands now, but my friends are still very busy.

❑ _____

❑ _____

❑ _____

❑ _____

About . . .

Notes to Family and Friends After a Loss

This activity will help you articulate anything you might want to say to family and/or friends. The mental fog associated with early mourning, and the heightened sensitivity that you may experience, can cause you to stuff your feelings or spew them inappropriately. It is important to communicate feelings, wishes, desires, hopes, dreams and disappointments with family and friends. This needs to be done with some selectivity and mature self-censorship.

This activity will help you rehearse what you are going to say. You may feel relief once you have written your message and no longer feel the need to say it, or the process may clarify just what needs to be said and how it can be done without burning bridges.

On the facing page . . .

Write your thoughts to articulate, or think through, what you want to say.

Then mail, email, call, tell them in person, keep in a 'remember' file to look back on, or discard.

After completing the activity. . .

Think about the people with whom you haven't been able to express your feelings and then journal why.

_____

_____

_____

_____

_____

_____

_____

_____

_____

_____

Notes to Family and Friends After a Loss

There might be things you would like to say to your family and friends and haven't been able to.

To	To
To	To
To	To

About . . .
Disappointed in your support system?

As people grieve, they often have expectations of their friends and family that are not met. Sometimes the expectations may be unreasonable; sometimes the family and friends are at a loss as to how to be supportive and/or helpful, for a multitude of possible reasons. It is important for you to acknowledge your disappointments.

Notice how your family members and friends have been behaving. Think about the changes that have occurred in relationships – is the behavior of the family member/friend really different than before the death of your loved one, or are you more sensitive to the same behavior now? Do you want, need or expect more? Have you considered that your family members and/or friends are also grieving, may not know what to say or do, feel inadequate, fear they have nothing to offer, or are frightened that the loss might happen to them?

On the facing page . . .

Fill in the grid regarding your disappointments.

After completing the activity . . .

Journal about the following questions:

- What disappointment have you felt in someone because that person hasn't been as supportive as you would like?

- What would you have liked them to do differently?

- Is that reasonable?

_____

_____

_____

_____

_____

_____

_____

_____

_____

Disappointed in your support system?

Often, other people mean well — but hurt our feelings.

	Who?	What this person did or didn't do.	What can I do about it?
Family			
Friends			
Clergy and/or Religious Community			
Physicians and/or Medical Staff			
Co-Workers			
Neighbors			

Remember, during grief, it is normal to be overly sensitive to others' behaviors.

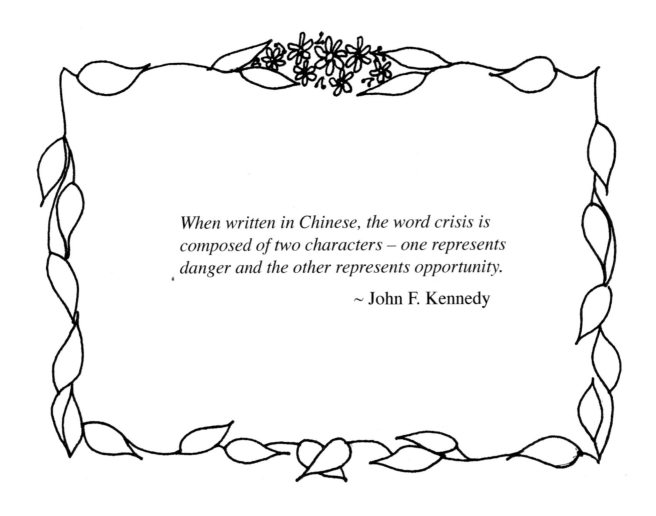

When written in Chinese, the word crisis is composed of two characters – one represents danger and the other represents opportunity.

~ John F. Kennedy

CHAPTER 6

Special Events

Special days – like holidays, birthdays, anniversaries, graduations, Sundays and many, many others – offer challenges to anyone who has suffered a loss. These days are glaring reminders (as if they were needed) of the absence of a loved one. You may find that your emotionality is heightened just prior, during and after any special day. Many people are surprised at this phenomenon and truly feel blindsided.

Another surprise that often catches people unaware is the emotional difficulty they experience during the second year following the loss. This is often true because people think that they have managed this particular event without the loved one, so it will be easier the second time. They do not prepare for the emotional impact and are shocked, or they realize, with hindsight, that during the particular event in the first year they were still quite numb, and in the second year they are fully experiencing their feelings.

This chapter is designed to heighten your awareness. Being alert in advance to some of these issues may improve the chance of handling the particular occasion with a greater degree of comfort.

About . . .
Coping with Special Days and Holidays

Holidays and special events like graduations, birthdays, anniversaries, etc. are very difficult to manage for newly bereaved people. Dealing with these major events can be challenging during the best of times. This page will help you anticipate the emotions that may be stirred up.

On the facing page . . .

Read this list of tips now and then refer to it prior to planning any special day or holiday.

After reading the page . . .

Have you thought about how you may honor family traditions and still do things differently?

Journal a possible conversation you might have with your family or others with whom you traditionally celebrate, about altering the usual way of doing things and symbolically bringing your loved one into the celebration.

_____

_____

_____

_____

_____

_____

_____

_____

_____

_____

_____

_____

Coping with Special Days and Holidays

Holidays and special events can be challenging and stressful times during the best of circumstances. They stir up memories of the past, evoke powerful feelings, and force us to compare our life situation to the past and/or to an idealized version.

Dealing with a holiday or special event after a death or loss can become even more difficult during and after the first year. Customary routines are ended, never to be repeated in quite the same way. Holidays can be significant, meaningful and enjoyable — and will be different.

HERE ARE SOME TIPS:

- Get plenty of rest.
- Set reasonable expectations for yourself. Don't try to do everything and see everyone.
- Be realistic about what can and cannot be done.
- Schedule brief breaks to be alone.
- Try to tell those around you what you really need, since they may not know how to help you. Ask for their understanding if you withdraw from an activity that doesn't feel like a good idea to you.
- Acknowledge to yourself that the occasion may be painful at times.
- Let yourself feel whatever you feel.
- Express feelings in a way that is not hurtful.
- Don't be afraid to rethink traditions. Keep in mind that traditions, even long-standing ones, can be changed and can be resumed next year, or not.
- Limit your time – grief is emotionally and physically exhausting.
- Take time for yourself for relaxation and remembrance.
- Honor the memory of a loved one – give a gift or donation in his or her name, light a candle, display pictures and/or share favorite stories with supportive people.
- Discuss, ahead of time with family and/or friends, what each person can do to make this time special. Share in the responsibility, and see what can be eliminated or included to keep it less stressful.
- If celebrating does not feel right, try volunteering this year.
- Think about what part of this event you are not looking forward to, and discuss with other participants ahead of time, what can be done to change it.
- Remember, it is okay to laugh and enjoy yourself.
- Leave an event early if you want or need to.
- Make a shopping list ahead of time and shop on a good day.
- Propose a toast to your loved one and invite people to share memories.
- Give yourself permission to cut back on holiday decorations, preparations and gift-giving.

Holidays and Special Events

Anticipating your reactions gives you an opportunity to plan in ways you might not have considered. This page will help you tap into your feelings and prepare for the bumps in the road of planning upcoming holidays and special events.

On the facing page . . .

Choose five of the sentence-starters and write in the first thoughts that come to your mind.

After completing the activity . . .

Think about an upcoming holiday or celebration and journal how you would like to spend that day.

_____

_____

_____

_____

_____

_____

_____

_____

_____

_____

_____

_____

_____

_____

Holidays and Special Events

My birthday _____ .

_____ .

On _____ , my concern is _____ .
      (holiday)

_____ .

Buying gifts is _____ .

_____ .

Special family events (graduations, weddings, births, etc.) are _____ .

_____ .

_____’s birthday is coming up soon and _____ .
     (name)

_____ .

On holidays I am still expected to _____ .

_____ .

Special events feel _____ .

_____ .

The anniversary of _____’s death will be coming soon and _____ .
     (name)

_____ .

_____ .

Funerals I feel obligated to attend _____ .

_____ .

The weekends _____ .

_____ .

Holiday Traditions

We often have idealized versions of how things used to be and how they *should* be. We usually fail to live up to that fantasy, especially at holiday time. Anticipating the stress of the holiday celebration gives you an opportunity to plan in ways you might not have considered. Even under usual circumstances, there is stress associated with holidays. Once a *New Normal* is established, new ways of dealing with holidays will emerge.

On the facing page . . .

In the first column, list the next major holiday. In the next column, list the traditions or routines you associate with the holiday. In the third column note what you anticipate to be stressful about these particular traditions or routines. Next, focus on possible changes you can make to minimize the stress. Any changes made now, are only for now. It may be appropriate to continue with the changes in the future, make other changes in the future or go back to the prior tradition. Those decisions can be made later.

After completing the activity . . .

Use this space to continue your list – or respond to –

What holiday creates the most stress in your life?
Journal what you can choose to do about it.

_____

_____

_____

_____

_____

_____

_____

_____

_____

_____

Holiday Traditions

It may be time to revise your holiday traditions.
Be kind to yourself and listen to your inner voice.

Holiday	In the Past Tradition / Routine	Stressors (family, finances, feelings, planning, etc.)	Possible Change of Tradition / Routine

Special Events Can Bring On Special Dilemmas

Anticipating difficult situations gives you an opportunity to think and plan. This activity will help you think about how to handle a variety of challenging situations.

On the facing page . . .

Put yourself in these situations and think about possible solutions.

After completing the activity . . .

Journal any additional sticky situation(s) you would like to work through.

_____

_____

_____

_____

_____

_____

_____

_____

_____

_____

_____

_____

_____

_____

_____

_____

_____

_____

Special Events Can Bring On Special Dilemmas

My husband recently died. A close relative invited me to her wedding. I think it will be difficult.

I could _____ .

My significant other died a year ago. I am invited out the night of our anniversary.

I could _____ .

In the middle of a holiday celebration, I start to cry.

I could _____ .

My child died. I'm invited to a school event by his best friend.

I could _____ .

A member of my family died and Thanksgiving is coming up. I don't think I want to celebrate the holiday but I think my family would be angry.

I could _____ .

My wife died. Every year I gave her something special for Valentine's Day. In February there are reminders of Valentine's Day wherever I go. I feel as if I should do something to mark the day but don't know what to do.

I could _____ .

The company where my recently deceased spouse worked is having their annual holiday party and invited me. They were so considerate to ask me, but I do not want to go.

I could _____

_____ .

About . . .

Not Looking Forward to the Weekends?

This activity applies primarily to people who have lost someone with whom they lived regularly. If this is your situation, you may find the weekends and evenings very difficult. You may be used to having your loved one around – someone to do things with, or for, and a general presence in your life. This activity will help you strategize ways to make the weekends better.

On the facing page . . .

Complete the sentence starters that focus on making the weekend better.

After completing the activity . . .

Journal about the most difficult time of the day or week for you and why.

_____

_____

_____

_____

_____

_____

_____

_____

_____

_____

_____

_____

_____

_____

_____

Not Looking Forward to the Weekends?

Activities I can plan to do on the weekend are _____

_____ .

A physical activity I could do is _____

_____ .

It's better if I avoid _____

_____ .

Productive things I could do are _____

_____ .

I can relax by _____

_____ .

I would look forward to _____

_____ .

It sounds like fun to _____

_____ .

Someone I can call is _____

_____ .

I can reorganize my weekly chores to _____

_____ .

I can pamper myself by _____

_____ .

I can plan an outing like _____

_____ .

_____

_____

_____

_____ .

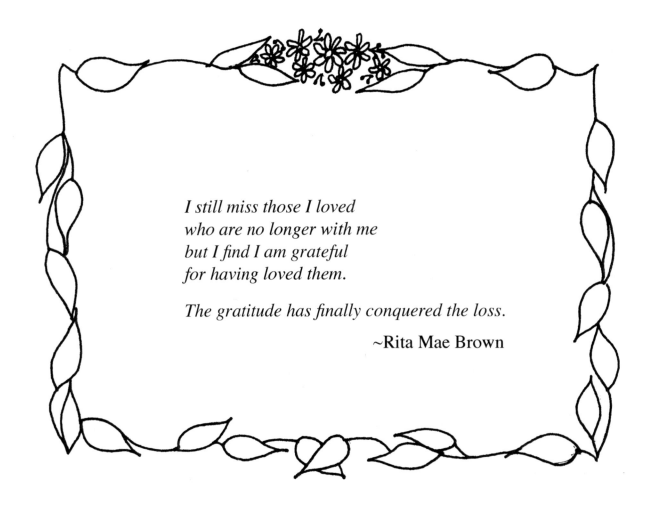

I still miss those I loved
who are no longer with me
but I find I am grateful
for having loved them.

The gratitude has finally conquered the loss.

~Rita Mae Brown

CHAPTER 7

A New Normal

Reorganizing one's life without the physical presence of the loved one is the hope and expectation we have for all of those who are grieving. This NEW NORMAL, like life itself, is filled with ups and downs, highs and lows, joys and sorrows. The focus of this chapter is to guide you toward the development of your NEW NORMAL with a full range of emotions.

By NEW NORMAL, we are consciously referring to each individual's own experience. NEW NORMAL is not a static destination and is unique to each individual. Each person has a unique way of being in the world. My NEW NORMAL will be *what is right for me*; your NEW NORMAL will be *what is right for you*. Developing a NEW NORMAL – a relatively comfortable way of living without the physical presence of the deceased – is the goal.

About . . .

Healing

This self-evaluation is a way to notice progress and develop awareness of areas that may still need work as you continue on your HEALING PATHWAY towards a NEW NORMAL. Review the THE HEALING PATHWAY, page 27, and the notion of a NEW NORMAL. Date the page and return to it at regular intervals. You may discover that you go back and forth along the path.

On the facing page . . .

Rate the questions 1, 2, 3, 4 or 5 to see where you are in the process.
(1 is **no way** and 5 is **absolutely**)

After completing the activity . . .

Choose one or both of these quotations and journal your thoughts.

It's not going to get better, but it will get different. ~ Mae R. Zelikow

Things may not be as good as they were, but they can still be pretty darn good.
~ Harry Rebell

_____

_____

_____

_____

_____

_____

_____

_____

_____

_____

_____

_____

Healing

Walking on THE HEALING PATHWAY
is an individual process because no
two people grieve in the same way.
Where are you on the THE HEALING PATHWAY?

Are you

____ forgiving yourself?

____ forgiving your loved one?

____ moving on with your life?

____ releasing uncomfortable emotions?

____ finding and accepting support?

____ taking care of yourself?

____ challenging yourself to learn new skills?

____ exercising?

____ spending time outdoors in nature?

____ scheduling and keeping health-care appointments?

____ surrounding yourself with supportive, positive people?

____ avoiding addictive behaviors?

____ contributing to society?

____ doing things that you enjoy?

____ giving and receiving hugs?

____ actively managing your stress?

____ listening to your inner-voice?

____ not worrying about pleasing others?

____ taking time to be alone?

____ keeping a balanced schedule?

____ TOTAL

The lowest possible total is 20.
The highest possible total is 100.

How do you think you are doing? _____

What Has Changed in My Life?

It is often helpful to notice what has changed. Some of the changes will feel very burdensome (I'm now living alone and I don't like it!), while others may feel like a weight has been lifted (I no longer need to visit the nursing home daily). Recognizing that life has changed and embracing the changes as part of the NEW NORMAL is a significant part of healing and accomplishing the task of moving forward.

On the facing page . . .

Fill in the grid. In addition to the sad, challenging and unpleasant changes, remember to include some positive and/or liberating changes.

After completing the activity . . .

Read the following and journal how it applies to you at this time.

For everything there is a season,
And a time for every matter under heaven:
A time to be born, and a time to die;
A time to plant, and a time to pluck up what is planted;
A time to kill, and a time to heal;
A time to break down, and a time to build up;
A time to weep, and a time to laugh;
A time to mourn, and a time to dance;
A time to throw away stones, and a time to gather stones together;
A time to embrace, and a time to refrain from embracing;
A time to seek, and a time to lose;
A time to keep, and a time to throw away;
A time to tear, and a time to sew;
A time to keep silence, and a time to speak;
A time to love, and a time to hate:
A time for war, and a time for peace.

~ Ecclesiastes 3:1-8

_____

_____

_____

_____

_____

What Has Changed in My Life?

	What Has Changed in My Life?	IT'S A GOOD THING!	IT'S NOT SUCH A GOOD THING!
1			
2			
3			
4			
5			
6			
7			
8			
9			
10			
11			
12			

About . . .
Empty House

This activity is designed particularly for anyone who lived with only one person who is no longer there.

Coming home to an empty house is a difficult part of the adjustment to the loss of a loved one, especially if that person was the only other person in the home. Re-creating a pleasing and inviting living space is important in the development of one's *NEW NORMAL*.

On the facing page . . .

Finish the two sentence starters and list other ideas at the bottom.

After completing the activity . . .

Journal your thoughts about these poignant words of Alan D. Wolfelt . . .

Death came without my permission.
While I know grief is universal, it's just so hard to contemplate
the death of someone who brought meaning to my life.

My life is in large part formed by the people around me.
Death creates the obvious - living without the presence of someone loved.
This dramatic change challenges my character, my personhood.

Learning to survive my changed life draws upon my resources.
I am still capable of being loved and cared for.
I am still capable of living a life of purpose and meaning.

_____

_____

_____

_____

_____

_____

_____

_____

Empty House

Going home or staying home can be difficult when a loved one is no longer there.

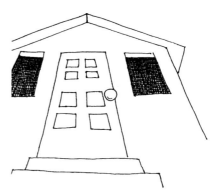

When I am home, I _____

_____

_____

_____

When I am away from the house and going back home, I_____

_____

_____

_____

How can I make the idea of being home or coming home more appealing?

- Turn the radio on before leaving to hear noise when coming home.
- Make a plan to do something enjoyable when I arrive home. (Work on a hobby or craft, watch a special television show, call a good friend or relative.)
- Adopt a pet to care for and greet me when I come home.
- Rearrange the furniture.

Other ideas:

_____

_____

_____

_____

_____

_____

About . . .

How can I honor _____?

Healing rituals are important ways that survivors can remember, in a concrete way, their loved one and continue the process of moving on. Rituals do not have to be religious or culturally specific; any remembrance activity can be considered a healing ritual.

On the facing page . . .

Consider ways to honor your loved one(s).

After completing the activity . . .

Journal what you have done to honor your loved one and how you feel about it.

_____

_____

_____

_____

_____

_____

_____

_____

What might be a ritual you would like to establish? Journal about it.

_____

_____

_____

_____

_____

_____

_____

How can I honor _____?

It is said that honoring a deceased person elevates that person's soul. It also helps us feel connected, especially if the manner in which we are honoring the person would be meaningful to that person. Honoring a loved one becomes a healing ritual for the survivors.

Here are some ways of honoring a loved one:

- Say a prayer on the anniversary of the death.
- Plant a tree.
- Give clothes to a charity.
- Sort through photos and put them in an album with comments written next to the pictures for the benefit of family members.
- Donate books to a school, university or public library.
- Volunteer time at a place in which the deceased had an interest.
- Establish a fund at a place of worship, favorite charity or college/school.
- Create and/or attend a memorial service.

Other ways I can honor my loved one:

- _____
- _____
- _____
- _____
- _____
- _____
- _____
- _____
- _____
- _____
- _____
- _____

About . . .

I loved just the way _____ was, however . . .
(name)

Often when a loved one dies the reaction is to idealize that person. Remembering the deceased person's flaws, eccentricities and habits is usually difficult. Sometimes feelings of disloyalty emerge.

On the facing page . . .

Completing the sentence starters will assist you in seeing the deceased as a complete person, warts and all. This is an indication of movement along THE HEALING PATHWAY.

After completing the activity . . .

Journal how it felt to do this activity.

_____

_____

_____

_____

_____

_____

_____

_____

_____

_____

_____

_____

_____

_____

_____

_____

_____

I loved just the way

_____
(name)

was, however . . .

I wish _____ .

Why didn't _____ .

If only _____ .

I hated it when _____ .

I am angry about _____ .

I wish _____ could have handled _____ .

I wonder why_____ didn't care about_____ .

Why wouldn't _____ .

and . . . _____

_____

_____

_____

_____

About . . .
LOOKING TOWARDS THE FUTURE

The general rule of thumb is that people who are grieving should not make any major decisions for a year. As with every other generalization, this is appropriate for some people, but not all. It is a sign of health and growth to be looking forward to, and beginning to imagine, what the future will be like without the physical presence of the deceased.

On the facing page . . .

Respond to the question, *One year from now, where do I want to be?* You can adapt it to imagine your future in shorter or longer time-frames. You need not take the time-frame literally.

After completing the activity . . .

Journal how it feels to envision your future without your loved one's physical presence – your NEW NORMAL.

_____

_____

_____

_____

_____

_____

_____

_____

_____

_____

_____

_____

_____

_____

LOOKING TOWARDS THE FUTURE

One year from today, where do I want to be?

Residence _____

Work _____

Learning _____

Leisure _____

Social _____

Relationships _____

Family _____

Healing _____

Spiritually _____

_____

_____

_____

_____

There is a promise of a brighter tomorrow!

About . . .
Moving Forward

Breaking goals down into small intermediate steps is helpful. Analyzing the barriers to completing each step is also a useful way to move forward to get things done. This activity will help you clarify actions to accomplish your goals.

On the facing page . . .

Think of one thing that you have wanted to do but have not done. Answer all of the questions on the facing page with that goal in mind.

After completing the activity . . .

Journal what doing this exercise was like for you and any insights you may have gained.

_____

_____

_____

_____

_____

_____

_____

_____

_____

_____

_____

_____

_____

_____

_____

_____

Moving Forward

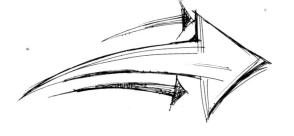

Can be overwhelming!
Breaking goals down into small steps is helpful.

What is a goal that you would like to accomplish, but you just can't get started?

_____

Is it necessary to do this immediately? _____

When would you like to get it done? _____

When would you want to start? _____

What is the first step in getting the goal accomplished? _____

_____

How long would that first step take? _____

When will you take the first step? _____

After the first step, when would you be willing to work on it again? _____

What would be the next step? _____

And the next? _____

And the next? _____

Would you like some support or would you prefer to do it alone? _____

If you would like help, who are a few people you would consider asking? _____

_____

How could you reward yourself each time you work on this project? _____

_____

When are you willing to begin?_____

About . . .
Affirmations

Affirmations are healing, positive statements that you say to yourself. They are also a way to counter negative self-talk. (Refer to *Self-Talk*, page 91)

Affirmations are most powerful when we can say them aloud to ourselves in a positive, confident way. Usually they are statements that, on some level, we *know* are true, but we often do not pay attention and sometimes do not believe. This is a way to shift our focus.

On the facing page . . .

Read the affirmations in the boxes. In the blank box, write your own personal affirmation. Copy the affirmations on index cards and place them on your bathroom mirror or dresser, dashboard of the car, desk at the office or at home; on the closet, bedroom or refrigerator doors; in your wallet or brief case, or in books used at home, work or school; or by the telephone. Look at them and repeat them throughout the day.

After completing the activity . . .

Read the following words of Elisabeth Kübler-Ross and then journal your thoughts.

> *LOVE*
> *. . . we . . . know that the absolutely only thing that matters is love. Everything else, our achievements, degrees, the money we made, how many mink coats we had, is totally irrelevant. It will also be understood that what we do is not important. The only thing that matters is how we do what we do. And the only thing that matters is that we do what we do with love.*

_____

_____

_____

_____

_____

_____

_____

_____

Affirmations

Affirmations are healing, positive statements you say to yourself.

I am moving to a NEW NORMAL.	*I have the ability to handle this.*
I am taking care of myself.	*I ask for help when I need it.*
I am a special person, unlike anyone else.	*I actually feel joyful at times.*
I am hopeful.	*I am surviving.*
I gain emotional strength each day.	

About . . .
I Have Choices

This activity will prompt you to think about the choices you have, the decisions you are making – and will continue to make – as you move forward. It is our intention to guide you to stop, think, and check in with yourself prior to making decisions. People make most of their decisions out of habitual thinking and reacting. Use this opportunity to help heighten awareness of these patterns and interrupt them.

On the facing page . . .

Identify one decision you are facing. List the wide variety of your choices. Use the questions on the facing page to help sort through all of your choices to make your decision. Check in with yourself as to what you want, and notice if you are making your choices based on love or fear. You are presently in a different circumstance and need to think about how you feel now, as opposed to how you used to think about this particular situation.

After completing the activity . . .

What is your reaction to Jean Nidetch's quotation?

It's choice – not chance – that determines your destiny.

How about Zig Zigler's quotation?

You are free to choose, but the choices you make today will determine what you will have, be, and do in the tomorrow of your life.

Journal your thoughts on either or both of these quotes.

_____

_____

_____

_____

_____

_____

_____

_____

I Have Choices

During a stressful period or disaster, the decision-making process can be greatly affected by our emotional responses to loss and grief. During this difficult time, many decisions may need to be made.

- Am I looking for what is right or am I looking for what is wrong?

- Am I making this decision based on my needs or am I trying to please someone else?

- Will this choice propel me toward a hopeful future or will it keep me stuck in the past?

- Will this choice bring me long-term fulfillment or short-term gratification?

- Will this choice increase or decrease my personal energy?

- Does this choice empower me or does it disempower me?

- Is this decision an act of self-love or is it an act of self-sabotage?

- Does this choice promote my personal growth?

- Is this an act of love or is it an act of fear?

A decision I need to make

_____

My choices

_____

_____

_____

To love oneself is the beginning
of a lifelong romance.
　　　　　　　　　~ Oscar Wilde

End Notes

Death is nothing at all,
I have only slipped away into the next room.
Whatever we were to each, that we are still.
Call me by my old familiar name.
Speak to me in the easy way which you always used.
Laugh as we always laughed
at the little jokes we enjoyed together.
Play, smile, think of me. Pray for me.
Let my name be the household word it always was.
Let it be spoken without effort.
Life means all that it ever meant.
It is the same as it always was;
There is absolutely unbroken continuity.
Why should I be out of your mind
Because I am out of your sight?

~ Henry Scott Holland

GriefWork Companion Reflections

We trust that completing this book has been useful for you, and helped you on your HEALING PATHWAY. It is our hope that you have been touched by this book and have developed a sense of yourself as learning, growing and loving in your NEW NORMAL. You may want to spend some time below and on the next page, reflecting on what you have learned through this process.

We would love to hear from you: **griefwork@ymail.com**.

Ester & Fran

_____

_____

_____

_____

_____

_____

_____

_____

_____

_____

_____

_____

_____

_____

_____

_____

_____

Additional Resources

Books

Creating Meaningful Ceremonies ~ by Alan D. Wolfelt

Disenfranchised Grief ~ by Kenneth J. Doka, Ph.D.

Grief Expressed ~ by Marta Felber

Grieving Mindfully ~ by Sameet M. Dumar

Hello from Heaven ~ Judy and Bill Guggenheim

Lessons of Loss ~ Robert Neimeyer

Life After Loss ~ by Raymond Moody Jr. & Dianne Arcangel

Love Lives On ~ by Louis LaGrand

Remembering Our Angels: Personal Stories of Healing from a Pregnancy Loss ~ by Hannah Stone

Mourning and Mitzvah ~ by Anne Brenner

Scribing the Soul, Essays in Journaling ~ by Kathleen Adams

The Grief Recovery Handbook: The Action Program for Moving Beyond, Death, Divorce, and other Losses ~ by John W. James and Russell Friedman

The Invisible String ~ Patrice Karst

The Journey Through Grief - Reflections on Healing ~ by Alan D. Wolfelt

The Next Place ~ by Warren Hanson

When Bad things Happen to Good People ~ by Harold Kushner

Widow to Widow ~ by Genevieve Davis Ginsburg

Winter Grief, Summer Grace ~ by James E. Miller

Web Sites

Alan D. Wolfelt, Ph.D., C.T. – Creating Meaningful Ceremonies
Center For Loss & Life Transition
    www.centerforloss.com

Elisabeth Kübler-Ross Foundation
    www.ekrfoundation.org

Belleruth Naparstek, LISW, BCD – Health Journeys
    www.HealthJourneys.com

Bill Guggenheim and Judy Guggenheim – After-Death Communications
    www.after-death.com

General Bereavement Information
    www.GriefNet.org

The Compassionate Friends
    www.thecompassionatefriends.org

© 2010 WHOLE PERSON ASSOCIATES, 101 W. 2ND ST., SUITE 203, DULUTH MN 55802 • 800-247-6789

Poems, Quotes, and Readings

Alphabetical Listing of Activity Pages